Dictations
for
Discussion

Second Edition

A Listening/Speaking Text

Judy DeFilippo
Catherine Sadow

PRO LINGUA  ASSOCIATES

Pro Lingua Associates, Publishers
P.O. Box 1348
Brattleboro, Vermont 05302 USA
Office: 802 257 7779
Orders: 800 366 4775
Email: info@ProLinguaAssociates.com
WebStore www.ProLinguaAssociates.com
SAN: 216-0579

*At **Pro Lingua***
our objective is to foster an approach
to learning and teaching that we call
***interplay,** the **intera**ction of language*
learners and teachers with their materials,
with the language and culture,
and with each other in active,
creative, and productive
play.

ISBN 13: 978-0-86647-317-0; 10: 10: 0-86647-317-3

Dictations for Discussion was designed by Arthur A. Burrows. It was set in Palatino, the most widely used, and pirated, face of the twentieth century, designed by Hermann Zapf in 1948 in Frankfurt. Although modern, it is based on Renaissance designs typical of the Palatinate area in Germany.

The photographs illustrating the book are from Dreamstime.com Agency: p. 1 © Ryan Rodrick Beiler, p. 4 © Rmarion, p. 8 © Howesjwe, p. 10 © Slavenkov Vukasovic, p. 16 © Perrypix, p. 27 © Andres Rodriguez, p. 32 © Daniel Zuckerkanel, p. 34 © Dmitry Dedyukhin, p. 37 © Atm2003, p. 45 © Sonja Gehrke, p. 46 © Diego Vito Cervo, p. 47 © Tracy Hornbrook, p. 49 © Monkey Business Images, p. 56 © Juriah Mosin, p. 74 © Gino Santa Maria, p. 79 © Dmitry Shironosov, p. 90 © Leigh Prather; © Petro Korchmar, p. 91 © Greenland, p. 92 © David Snyder, p. 93 © Rostislav Adamovsky, p. 98 © Suzanne Tucker; © Janks, p. 105 © Brett Rabideau, p. 107 Jjspring, p. 108 © Joao Virissimo, p. 110 © Bjeayes, p. 114 © Leahkat, p. 118 © Jun He, p. 120 © Ron Iscoff, p. 121 © Tramontana, p. 122 © Valdore, p. 120 © Nomadsoul1, p. 129 © Hana-svitlana Oliynyk, p. 132 © Hugo Maes, p. 134 © Robert Young, p. 137 © Zenpix, p. 142 © Irkusnya, p. 146 © Pancaketom, p. 151 © Jill Battaglia, p. 152 © Shakeyimages, p. 154 © Bosnok, p. 157 © Sergey Rusakov, p. 161 © Halina Yakushevich, p. 163 © Mark Fairey, p. 164 © Timur Djafarov, p. 167 Hallgerd, p. 170 © Paul Maguire, © Rmarion, p. 171 © Yukata, p. 172 © Ghubonamin, p. 175 © Alexander Sviridenkov, p. 178 © Brian Finestone, p. 181 © Sinisa Botas, p. 182 © Paul Prescott, p. 185 © Shuttlecock, p. 187 © Stuart Monk, p. 188 © Sebastian Czapnik, p. 189 © Poznyakov, p. 197 © Eric Inghels, p. 200 © Phartisan, p. 203 © Madartists, p. 207 © Suhendri Utet. Elements of some art were drawn from Googlepix and other online sources. Graphic for *Help for Haiti Now* p. 183 © hopeforhaitinow.org–CMT.com Clipart illustrating the book is from *The Big Box of Art,* Copyright © 2001 Hemera Technologies Inc., and *Art Explosion 750,000 Images,* Copyright © 1995-2000 Nova Development Corporation. Portrait of Bono p. 83 by Suzi Vaine. Cover photo of Kilauea Volcano in Hawaii © Pasojo: Dreamstime.com

The book was printed and bound by McNaughton & Gunn in Saline, Michigan.

Printed in the United States of America
Second edition, second printing 2013. 6400 copies in print.

Contents

Contents, *continued*

Acknowledgements

The authors based many of their activities on concepts introduced by P. Davis and M. Rinvolucri, who co-authored *Dictation, New Methods, New Possibilities*, Cambridge University Press, 1988.

The authors are grateful to the authors, publishers, and others who have given permission to reprint copyrighted materials:

American Psychological Association: *Sexual Orientation*

The Associated Press: *Marriage; Wedded Fiscal Bliss,* D. Crary

The Boston Globe

Photo of Dogs, Paul Baker

Concerns Over Increasing U.S. Birthweights, Douglas Bekin

As U.S. Obesity Rises, Karen Hsu

Deep Pockets Are In, Cindy Rodriguez

Older Learner's Graduation an Inspiration, Victoria Benning

Lucky Dishes for New Year, Bonnie Tsui

Three Little Words, Erma Bombeck; The Aaron Priest Literary Agency

Obituary of Ruth Rothfarb, Tom Long

Eating Smart, Jean Kressy

Clone Research, Raja Mishra

Center for Counseling and Student Development at Northeastern University: *Facts on Drinking*

Creators Syndicate: Ann Landers Permission

David Muir and Pressman Toys: cards from *Judge for Yourself*

The Economist: *A World Empire by Other Means*

The Internet: *How's Your Mental Health?* AskpsychMD.com by Mark Faber, MD

Open Adoption, Bill and Eve Kuhlemeier Website

Various sources: *Phishing, Babe Didrikson Zaharias, Idioms for Test Takers, Natural Disasters, Tax Quiz, All About Ice Cream, Bono, Hanging Out to Dry, Learning Styles*

The New York Times: *Stroked, Poked, and Hypnotized* by D. Wilkinson; *Hold the Pickles–Hold the Lettuce* by M. Kakutani

The Northeastern News: *Trials of Tipping*

Oceana Publications, Inc.: *Election Day,* M. B. Lorenz

The Patriot Ledger: *Cheating,* Dina Gerdeman; *There's No Purr-fect Answer,* D. Conkey

Simon and Schuster: *The Psychology of Shopping,* Paco Underhill

USA Today: *Answering the Need to Help,* Perry Flicker

Workman Publishers: *Family Reunion*

In memory of
Edgar Sather

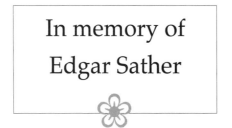

Introduction

Dictations for Discussion is an intermediate-to-advanced-level text that is intended to improve the listening and speaking skills of ESL students. Reading and writing are also reinforced, along with progress in vocabulary and grammar. This text provides a wide variety of dictations from authentic materials that include provocative news items, problems to solve, and decisions to make.

The units are designed to stand alone so that teachers can pick and choose which dictations meet the needs, interests, and levels of their students. Each unit begins with a short introduction that provides a background and context for the dictation. The central focus of the unit is a dictation activity followed by a discussion section. The discussions can take place in pairs or small groups. The unit ends with a follow-up activity which is intended to explore the topic further through writing, research, and speaking activities. This text includes several cooperative learning activities.

Most units are two or three pages long. Some units will take less time than others, so a shorter unit or part of a unit can be done as a fill-in. The dictations can take between 15 and 20 minutes, and the discussions can take from 20 to 30 minutes. Some follow-up activities can be done in class and others can be done out of class.

The complete texts of the dictations begin on page 137. These full texts can be read to the students or a student can read them to the class. They are also available on two CDs.

❀ Types of Dictation ❀

Dictation has been presented in many forms through the years in reading, listening, grammar, and writing classes. It is also used as an assessment procedure. This text, however, does not deal with scoring or analyzing student work. The dictations are meant to be a challenging and open springboard to discussion in which students are encouraged to use the language they have just learned.

This text includes five types of dictation: partial, pair, dictogloss, note-taking, and prediction. While all units include pair and group work in the discussion segments, several units will include more extensive cooperative activities. See the unit on "Birthdays Around the World" as an example.

Partial Dictation (sometimes known as cloze) ❈

Most of the dictations in this text are partial dictations where words, phrases, or chunks of language have been deleted, and students are required to listen and write down the missing words. All the dictations should be discussed upon completion. Pair work is encouraged.

Pair Dictation (sometimes known as mutual) ❈

This dictation requires students to work in pairs to combine two-part texts into one continuous piece. One student has a copy of dictation Part A, and the other has dictation Part B. Each student has half of the text. They should not look at each other's sheets. They take turns. Student A dictates and B writes; then B dictates and A writes, and so on until the story is complete.

Dictogloss ❈

In this kind of dictation, the focus is on getting the main idea of a sentence or short paragraph. There are many variations of the dictogloss technique. In the directions for the sentence-level dictogloss, students are told that they will hear a sentence only once, after which they are to jot down the words they can recall and try to reconstruct the sentence in writing as accurately as they can. The first time this is done, the teacher will probably have to allow the students a second reading until they discover that they need to pay attention the first time around. As the students work at rebuilding the sentence, they can work in pairs and then fours.

Note Taking ❈

Note-taking activities require students to write down information they think is important for the discussion that follows. This may only amount to a few words; however, when students work in pairs after the listening section is over, they should compare their notes to be sure they caught the pertinent information. When this is accomplished, they are able to discuss the issues that follow.

Prediction Dictation ❈

Prediction lessons come in two parts. The first part focuses more on reading skills and grammar. The students are required to work in pairs, reading the passage, and predicting (or guessing) what should be in each blank space. Any logical and grammatically correct word or phrase can be accepted. Part Two requires the students to listen to the same passage and see if their guesses were correct, or similar.

❊ Tips for Teachers ❊

1. When reading the full dictations, try to speak naturally, at normal speed, keeping the features of the spoken language. If you are reading the full text at normal speed and you know the exercise will be fairly easy for your students, give the word, phrase, or chunk of language only once. Try to start at a pace that is comfortable for your students, and then make them work a bit at understanding. If you think the text will be difficult for the students, repeat two, possibly three times. When field-testing our material, several teachers said they thought the material looked quite difficult for their students, but they were surprised at how well the students did. It's up to you to decide what works best. If you have to repeat more than three times, the text is too difficult for the students.

2. The students may want to check the spelling of a word or words as you are giving the dictation. It's best to tell them to wait until the end of the activity.

3. For numbers, have the students write numerals, rather than the word (15, instead of fifteen), except for single-digit numbers (1-9). They should also use dollar ($) and percentage symbols (%), rather than writing out the words.

4. One key to making the dictation a positive experience is to have students correct their own work. When the dictation is completed, the students check with each other in pairs on what they've heard as you walk around helping and clarifying. This, in itself, allows for a great deal of discussion. After they have self-corrected, they can turn to the full dictation texts for confirmation. You can then go over the dictation with the class and discuss whatever vocabulary or concepts they don't understand.

5. Rather than read the dictations from the appendix, you may find it helpful to copy the page you're dictating and fill in the blanks yourself ahead of time. This is helpful when giving feedback. It's easier when you're working from the same page as your students. Here is an example:

    > Cheating in the classroom isn't just about _copying_ someone's paper or writing answers on a _crib sheet_. With the _Internet_, cheating has gone _high tech_.

6. There was no pattern that was followed when choosing words or phrases to be deleted. Sometimes the deletions focus on idioms, sometimes on numbers, sometimes grammar, sometimes vocabulary.

7. *Dictations for Discussion* also works well for substitute teachers, since a minimum amount of preparation is needed.

8. You and your students can also create dictations from local newspapers, the Internet, or any other source. This way you can choose a timely topic and easily adapt it to the level of your students.

9. With more advanced students, you may want to ask a student to give a dictation by reading from the full dictations. The reader may prepare for this by listening to the CD.

10. The photographs used throughout the book have been chosen to be used as prompts for more discussion.

11. **Cooperative activities** have been included in three of the units. These are extensions of pair and group work and they are one of the best ways to have everyone in the class very involved:

Day 1.

There are four groups, A, B, C, and D. Everyone in each group is responsible for researching part of the material assigned to that group.

Day 2.

All groups reassemble, and the group members go over all the information they have gathered, being sure that each member is fully familiar with all the material.

Day 2 or 3.

New groups are formed. Each group includes one person from each of the original groups. In other words, each new group will consist of one A, one B, one C, and one D. The Group A person is responsible for sharing all of the Group A material. By the end of this activity every member of the class should have the complete information. This can be a lengthy activity, but it is very valuable, especially for shyer students.

❀ Using the CDs ❀

Although it is not necessary to have and use the accompanying CDs, many teachers find that having the CDs provides greater flexibility in using the material. They can be used in several ways:

1. Play the track once through without stopping before reading the dictation to the students. This will introduce the topic and give the students a head start toward comprehending the dictation when it is read to them.

2. To give the students a chance to hear a different voice, have the students take the dictation from the CD. Although more challenging, this can help the students prepare for standardized listening tests. You can use the pause button; that will allow the students time to fill in the blanks.

3. Play the CD after the students have taken the dictation and checked their answers. This can help the students improve and become more confident in listening comprehension.

On the CDs, each dictation text is on a separate track. The CD track numbers are given in the table of contents of this book (iii-iv), and also next to the titles of the gapped texts (1-135) and the titles of full dictations texts (137-209).

❀ Using a Media/Listening Laboratory ❀

Almost any dictation that is done in class can also be done in a media/listening lab. However, there are some additional things that can be done in the lab that cannot be done in a classroom.

1. Read a short partial dictation in the lab. Then have the students record what they have written. You can collect both, and then on the student CD, give some feedback on their pronunciation.

2. Have the students create their own partial dictation and make four or five copies of it. They record it carefully and leave the results at their stations. They then move from station to station doing four or five of each other's dictations. The students' dictations can follow a general theme – food, for example, or a specific form – a joke or poem.

3. Dictate a chunk of language. Have the students listen and record it. Add another chunk. Let the students record again. At the end of the short, fairly simple dictation, the students transcribe it. Collect their transcriptions and make appropriate comments and corrections.

4. Dictate a problem. An example might be a "Dear Abby" letter that you have turned into a dictation. After each student has done the dictation, they record the solution to the problem. You should listen and respond to the solution, or the students can move from station to station listening to their fellow students and making comments of agreement or disagreement. By preparing short, easy-to-understand dictations first, you can also use this technique to introduce current political or social topics that you think will be of particular interest to your students.

❀ About the Full Dictation Texts ❀

The complete texts for the dictations begin on page 137. They are recorded on two CDs, or you can read these full texts to give the dictations.

Dictations
for
Discussion

Immigration Statistics

Introduction ❀

Immigration has been a major source of population growth and cultural change through-out much of American history. Since the founding of the U.S., more than 62 million immigrants from every continent have settled here. Since the liberalization of immigration policy in 1965, the number of first-generation immigrants living in the U.S. has quadrupled from 9.6 million in 1970 to about 38 million in 2007. The population of the U.S. in 2010: 308,000,000.

Dictation ❀ *Write the correct word or number in the blank space. Correct and discuss the dictation. The USCIS stands for U.S. Citizenship and Immigration Service.*

1. _____ _____ _____ an average of more than ___ _____

   _____, legal and _____, settled in the U.S. each year.

2. Legal immigration _____ between _____ and _____

   each year, and the USCIS estimates that _____ _____

   _____ settle here each year. Most illegal immigrants are from Mexico.

3. In 2008, a record _____ legal immigrants were naturalized

   as U.S. _____.

4. _____ _____ _____ of legal immigrants to come between

   2001 and 2009 came from _____, _____, the Philippines,

   and _____.

5. The Census Bureau projects that ____ _____, one quarter _____ _____

   _____ will be of _____ _____.

6. In California, home to over _____ _____ Asian-Americans, _____ of all

   Californians are working for _____-_____ businesses or paying

   rent to an _____ _____.

Discussion ❀ *Discuss these questions with a partner. Share your ideas with the class.*

1. What groups of immigrants can be found in your country?
2. What kind of work can they find?
3. Do they suffer from discrimination? If yes, in what ways?
4. Can they become citizens? How long does it take to become one?

Follow up ❀ *Write a paragraph giving reasons why immigrants leave their country of origin.*

Open Adoption

(CD 1 TRACK 2) ♦ *[FULL TEXT 138]*

Introduction ❀

Open adoption is a legal process where the biological parents, called birthparents, not only choose the adoptive parents but also remain in contact with their child and his/her parents. People who select open adoption believe that it is important for the birthparents to know how their child is doing and for the child to have direct access to information and support from the birthparents. It is a unique partnership with separate and distinct roles. In the dictation you will hear an interview with a mother and father who share their experience as adoptive parents of two sons.

Dictation ❀ *Write the correct word or number in the blank space. Correct and discuss the dictation.*

Q. Why did you choose an open adoption?

A. This is a big question, but it _____ _____ _____ _____ ; once

we got over the fear that everyone seems to have at first, we _____

_____ _____ of openness. Without the secrecy involved in traditional,

_____ _____ adoption, there will never be the questions of: "Why

did my birthmom _____ _____ _____?" Or, "I wonder

_____ _____ to my baby?" Or, "_____ _____ _____

_____?" Or, "What kind of woman _____ _____ to this child?"

When there are answers _____ _____ _____, it's better and

healthier for everyone.

Q. Aren't you worried that the birthmom will want her baby back?

A. _____ _____ _____ _____ of the agency we went with, is the

excellent counseling that was provided to both us and our children's birthmoms.

_____ ____ _____ of this counseling, we were all comfortable with our

_____ _____ _____.

Because of this comfort, _____ _____ _____ _____ of a reclaim

situation. Also, we knew that the agency we used followed the _____

_____ and provided for a fairly secure relinquishment of

_____ _____ _____. This was the only way we

_____ _____ _____ doing our second adoption.

Q. Are you going to maintain contact with your sons' birthmoms?

A. Yes, we have a very _____ _____ with our sons'

birthmoms. We live _____ _____ to Will's birthmom and visit

_____. We have been to Will's _____-_____ birthday party,

and they came to Will's first birthday party. We _____ _____ email

and cards. Our sons will always have their _____ in _____

_____, as well as another set of _____! (There's

_____ _____ _____ as too many Grandmas and

Grandpas!) Many people seem to think that _____ _____

involved would _____ _____ _____-_____ or maybe

a step-parent relationship. This _____ _____ _____ _____. We are

the "_____ and _____" parents of our children.

Discussion ❀ _Discuss these questions with a partner. Share your ideas with the class._

1. Is adoption common in your culture? Is open adoption an option? How do you feel about adoption?

2. Why would a person give up a child for adoption?

Discussion ❦ *Read the situations. Discuss the questions with a partner. Share your ideas with the class.*

Situation 1:

Meg Harris, who is happily married with two children, was adopted 40 years ago and has wonderful parents. But she always had questions that bothered her for many years and started a ten-month search for her birthparents. By law, any adopted child can seek biological parents. She discovered that her father had recently died and left no family. She was excited when she located her birthmother but was bitterly disappointed when her mother refused to see her. Her mother was married and hadn't told her two adult children about Meg, and didn't want them to know.

Was Meg's biological mother wise not to meet with her? Why or why not?
What questions do you think Meg would want to ask her biological parents?

Situation 2:

In their 40 years of marriage, Carol and Bob Deering have adopted more than 25 disabled children, now ranging in ages from 10 to 33. They believe that all children deserve a loving home, and they take the kids that most people don't want or can't handle. The children are Black, White, Asian, and Latino, but all have some kind of physical or mental disability. For example, they adopt children with cerebral palsy, brain damage, or Down Syndrome. Many had mothers who were drug abusers. Some suffered physical abuse. In their large New York home the Deerings currently have six young adults living with them.

What qualities do the Deerings have to have in order to deal with these children?
Would you consider adopting a disabled child?

Follow up ❦ *Write a paragraph to explain* **one** *of the following questions:*

1. Adoptive parents are advised to tell their children that they are adopted as soon as they can understand what adoption means. Why is this advice usually followed?
2. What do you know about adoption in your own or another country?

Sexual Orientation: Questions and Answers

(CD 1 track 3) ♦ *[Full Text 140]*

Introduction ❀

Issues surrounding the topic of homosexuality have sparked emotional debate in many countries around the world. In the United States, homosexuality has been a political and legal issue in the nation's capitol, in state legislatures, and in the courts. In this question and answer format, we hope to address some of the misconceptions that may exist. Before you listen, check the meaning of the following sexual orientations:

1. *Heterosexuality:* a sexual attraction to a person of the opposite sex. A heterosexual is often referred to as a straight person.

2. *Homosexuality:* a sexual attraction to a person of the same sex.
   a. Gay is a synonym for homosexual.
   b. A lesbian is a homosexual woman.

3. *Bisexuality*: a sexual attraction to both men and women.

Dictation ❀ *Write the correct word or number in the blank space. Correct and discuss the dictation.*

1. What is sexual orientation?

   Sexual orientation is an emotional, _____, or sexual attraction

   to another person. It includes heterosexuality, homosexuality, and various forms of

   _____. Most scientists today agree that _____

   _____ is most likely the result of a complex interaction of

   _____, cognitive, and environmental factors. In most people, sexual

   orientation is shaped _____ _____ _____ _____.

2. Is sexual orientation a choice?

   No. Human beings cannot choose to be either _____ or _____.

   Mental health professionals do not consider sexual orientation to be a _____

   _____. There is considerable evidence to suggest that biology, including

   _____ or _____ hormonal factors, plays a significant role in a person's

   sexuality.

3. Can therapy change sexual orientation?

   No. Even though most homosexuals live _____, _____ lives, some

   homosexual or bisexual people may seek to change their sexual orientation through

   therapy because they are often _____ by family members or religious

   groups to try andto do so. _____ _____ _____ that homosexuality is not an

   illness. It does not require treatment and _____ _____ _____.

4. Is homosexuality a mental disorder or emotional problem?

   No. Psychologists and other _____ _____ professionals agree that it is

   not an illness, mental _____, or emotional problem. _____

   _____ is based on 35 years of objective, well-designed research.

5. Why is it important for society to be better educated about homosexuality?

   _____ _____ _____ about sexual orientation and

   homosexuality is likely to diminish _____–_____ _____.

   Accurate information is especially important to young people who are first discovering

   and _____ to _____ their sexuality – whether

   homosexual, bisexual, or heterosexual.

6. Is there any legislation against anti-gay violence?

   Yes. Some states include violence _____ _____ _____ on

   the basis of his or her sexual orientation as a "_____ _____," and

   ten U.S. states have laws against discrimination _____ _____

   _____ _____ sexual orientation.

Family Gay and Lesbian Pride Parade in Vancouver, BC, Canada

Discussion ❀ *Discuss these questions with a partner. Share your ideas with the class.*

1. Homosexuals are in every occupation – from doctors, football players, and hair stylists to teachers. Are there certain professions that are more accepting of homosexuals? Some gays are open about their lifestyle and others are "in the closet." Why do some homosexuals prefer to stay in the closet?

2. There are currently as many as eight million lesbian mothers and gay fathers in the United States. The majority of their children are from previous heterosexual marriages. Why do you think a gay man and woman would marry a heterosexual when these marriages almost always end in divorce?

3. The American Academy of Pediatrics has recently endorsed the right of gay couples to adopt children. Why do you think this organization is now endorsing this kind of adoption?

4. There are countries in the world that still treat homosexuality as a crime or as a disease. Do you know of any countries that do this?

Follow up ❀ *Write a paragraph on* **one** *of the following items.*

1. Your 14-year-old brother confides in you that he is gay. How do you respond to him?
2. Same-sex marriage is now legal in many states. Why have the courts decided on this?

The Psychology of Shopping

(CD 1 TRACK 4) ♦ [FULL TEXT 141]

Introduction ❀

We shop for necessities. We also shop for many other reasons. The psychology of shoppers is carefully studied by marketers and the advertising industry. If you're a shopper, you probably already know a lot about the psychology of shopping.

Dictation ❀ *Below are some statements about shopping. After completing the dictation, decide if each of the statements is True or False.*

__ 1. Market research _____ _____ that the _____ _____ _____ makes customers feel like spending money.

__ 2. Upon entering a store, most customers head _____ _____.

__ 3. The only reason _____ _____ _____ is that they need something.

__ 4. Women have _____ _____ _____ for shopping than men.

__ 5. Express lines _____ _____ to reduce _____ _____.

__ 6. Online shopping is for the middle and upper classes because you must have a _____, _____ _____ _____, and a _____ ____.

__ 7. _____ are _____ _____ _____ _____ bought most online.

__ 8. Men purchase or influence purchases _____ _____ _____ _____ of all purchases and services.

__ 9. Studies show that most people are much less likely to buy, _____ _____ _____ _____ _____ as much when paying with cash _____ _____ _____ a credit card.

__ 10. When two women shop together, they often spend less time and money than _____ _____ _____ _____.

Discussion ❀ *After checking the dictation, discuss the following questions with a partner.*

1. According to psychologists, we shop for many reasons. Can you and your partner think of four or five reasons why we shop?

2. How is shopping different in two countries that you have lived in?

3. Do you sometimes buy things that you hadn't planned on buying? This is called "impulse buying." Tell your partner about one of your impulse purchases.

4. Are you very pleased when you buy something "on sale"? Give an example of a great bargain that you got.

5. Do you prefer to shop alone or with someone?

6. Have you ever bought anything on the Internet? Talk or write about a good or bad experience you've had with Internet shopping. Do you think Internet shopping will eventually become the only way we shop?

Follow up ❀ *Choose* **one** *of the following topics to write about.*

1. Write about one of the best shopping experiences you have had or one of the worst shopping experiences you have had.

2. If you had the opportunity to open a small store, what kind of store would you open? Write about it, and be specific about where it would be, who your customers would be, and what you would sell.

3. Write about the advantages and disadvantages of shopping on the Internet.

English Pronunciation and Spelling

(CD 1 TRACK 5) ♦ [FULL TEXT 142]

Introduction ❀

English has some of the most complicated spelling rules of any written language. For instance "slow" "dough" and "go" rhyme despite having different letter endings. Also even though "dough" and "rough" are spelled almost exactly the same, they are pronounced differently. Every few years there is a movement to change the spelling of many words, but nothing ever happens.

Dictation ❀ *All of these sentences have words that are spelled the same but are pronounced differently and have different meanings. Fill in the blank spaces with the word or words you hear. Repeat the sentences after your teacher says them and then practice them with your partner.*

1. They are too _____ to the door to _____ it.

2. There was a _____ among the oarsmen about how to _____.

3. I shed a _____ about the _____ in my new shirt.

4. A farmer can _____ _____.

5. The dump was so full it had to _____ _____.

6. The _____ is a good time to _____ the _____.

7. The insurance for the _____ was _____.

8. The bandage was _____ around the _____.

9. The soldier decided to _____ in the _____.

Discussion ❀ *Discuss the following questions with your partner.*

1. Can you think of similar pairs of words in English?

2. Can you think of other words that cause pronunciation problems in English?

3. What are your biggest pronunciation problems when speaking English?

4. What pronunciation problems do people who are learning your first language have?

Follow up ❀ *List words in English with spellings that you have had problems with.*

Phishing

(CD 1 track 6) ♦ *[Full Text 143]*

Introduction ❀

Phishing is an Internet crime. It's the email you might receive that falsely claims to be a legitimate business in an attempt to scam the user into giving *personal and financial* information. Here are some facts and warnings for you, the Internet user.

Dictation ❀ *Listen and fill in the blanks with the word or words you hear.*

1. _____ _____ to email or pop-up messages that ask for personal or financial information, and _____ _____ ____ _____ in the message. Don't _____ _____ _____ a link from the message into your Web browser because phishers _____ _____ _____ _____ _____ _____ _____ _____ _____ _____ _____ _____ but actually send you to a different site.

2. Some scammers send an email that _____ ____ _____ from a legitimate business and ask you to call a phone number to _____ _____ _____ or access a "_____." Don't call this number. If you need to reach an organization _____ ____ _____ _____, call the number on your financial statements or ____ _____ _____ ____ _____ _____ _____.

3. Use _____-_____ software and anti-spyware as well as a firewall, and update them regularly.

4. Review credit card and _____ _____ _____ as soon as you receive them to check for _____ _____.

5. Be careful about opening ____ _____ or downloading any files from emails you receive, regardless of who sent them.

6. _____ _____ _____ to: spam@uce.gov or reportphishing@antiphishing.org

Discussion ❀

Here is an example of a phishing email. It looks official but it is from a fictional bank. Check for spelling mistakes and incorrect grammar, which are common in most phishing emails. Also note that although the URL of the bank's webpage appears to be legitimate, it actually links to the phisher's web page.

Dear Valued Customer of Trusted Bank,

We have recieved notice that you have recently attempted to withdraw the following amount from your checking account in another country: $135.25.

If this information not correct, someone unknown may have access your account. As a safety measure, please visit our website via the link below to verify your personel information.

http://www.trustedbank.com/general/cust.verifyinfo.asp

Once you have done this, our fraud department will work to resolve this discrepency. We are happy you have chosen us to do business with.

Thank you,
TrustedBank   Member FDIC 2011, TrustedBank, Inc.

With a partner, discuss these items from the "Trusted Bank email."

1. What words and phrases should you be careful of?
2. What grammar and spelling mistakes can you find?
3. What words and phrases sound legitimate to you?
4. If you click on the website address, what will happen?
5. How can you find out if this is a legitimate email or not?

Follow up ❀ *Visit the Federal Trade Commission's Identity Theft website at* ftc.gov/idtheft *to find out more.*

Tax Quiz

(CD 1 TRACK 7) ♦ *[FULL TEXT 144]*

Introduction ❀

Americans say that there are two guarantees in life: death and taxes. The federal government taxes income as its main source of revenue. Most states also tax income. Of all the rituals of American life, none is more certain than filling out yearly income tax forms.

Dictation ❀ *Fill in the blank spaces with the word or words you hear. Then choose the answer you think is correct. Guess if you don't know.*

1. What percent _____ _____ _____ does an average American

   working couple pay in taxes _____ _____?

   a. 38%   b. 25%   c. 12%   d. 59%

2. The United States is the country with _____ _____ _____. True or False?

3. Where you live _____ _____ the amount of tax you pay. True or False?

4. _____ _____ pays the most in income tax?

   a. single and young   b. married and middle-aged   c. old

5. _____ _____ _____ _____ _____ do most of the U.S. income

   taxes come?

   a. People with a salary below $25,000 a year

   b. People with a salary between $25,000 and 50,000

   c. People with a salary above $50,000

6. People making the same income _____ _____ _____ _____ _____.

   True or False?

7. _____ _____ _____ of American tax dollars goes to

   a. national defense   b. health and Medicare   c. transportation

8. Denmark is a country with very high income taxes but it also enjoys _____

   _____ and _____ _____ _____.

   True or False?

Discussion 1 ❁ *Work with a partner and discuss these questions.*

1. In the dictation quiz, what surprised you the most? Why?

2. Two ways of collecting income tax are a graduated income tax and a flat-rate tax. A graduated tax is based on the idea that the more money you make, the more taxes you pay. A flat-rate income tax means that everyone pays the same percent. In Massachusetts, for example, workers pay 6%. Therefore, a person who makes $25,000 a year and a person who makes $100,000 a year will both pay 6%. Which tax is more equitable? Why?

3. Can you name some countries where citizens pay income taxes of more than 44%?

4. Can you name some countries where there are no taxes? Where does the government get the money to pay for public services?

5. Can you name some other types of taxes that Americans pay in addition to income taxes?

Discussion 2 ❁ *Here is a weekly pay stub for Ellen Thompson's work. With a partner, ask each other questions. Then answer them.*

936840		NON-NEGOTIABLE RETAIN FOR YOUR RECORDS				DESCRIPTION		CURRENT	
ADJ. SALARY	TAXES	DEDUCTIONS		NET PAY		REGULAR SALARY		1295	16
1088 66	374 66			*713	91	PENSION		103	61
						MEDICAL INS.		102	89
SOC. SEC. NO.				EXEMPTIONS		ADJSTED SALARY		1088	66
				FED.	STATE	FEDERAL TAX		229	24
108-30-9665				01	01	FICA		91	21
						MASS TAX		54	30
MO. DAY YEAR									
06 15 16									
		ELLEN THOMPSON 23 TOWER LANE BEDFORD, MA 01730				NET PAY		**713	91
SPRINGFIELD QUALITY CONTROL									

Follow up ❁ *Calculate the following items.*

1. Let's say that the sales tax in your state is 6%.
   If you bought a_____ how much sales tax would you pay?

   a. new car for $15,500   b. new TV for $670   c. new sofa for $940

2. Let's say that the income tax rate (flat rate) in your state is 4.5%. Your salary is $900 per week. How much would your state take out of your paycheck?

Trivia Contest

(CD 1 track 8) ♦ *[Full Text 146]*

Introduction ❧

A contest is a game with winners and losers. Trivia is defined as information that is not important but is often fun to know.

Dictation ❧

After you fill in the blank spaces, work together in groups of three – quietly so other groups don't hear your answers – and answer as many questions as you can. Guess if you don't know. Assign one person as secretary to write down your answers. Your teacher will come around to each group to get your answers. The group with the most correct answers wins!

1. How many people are there in _____ _____?

2. Where are most American cars _____ in the United States?

3. _____ _____ are presidential _____ _____ in the U.S?

4. Who wrote The _____ of Huckleberry _____?

5. What does ____ ____ ____ mean? (Hint: it's a kind of sandwich)

6. Where can you buy a _____ _____?

7. Who is the _____ _____ in the world?

Lunar Module LM-13
Astronaut Cradle of Aviation

8. In what year did Americans _____ _____ on the moon?

9. What is the _____ _____ first name in the world? (Hint: it's not an American name)

10. What is the _____ – _____ ice cream _____ in the U.S.?

11. How long has your teacher _____ in this program?

Cooperative Learning ❀

Work in four groups of three or four students. Using the Internet, each student finds out about one or more items listed below and reports back to the group. Then all four groups present what they have learned. Point out the locations on a world map.

Group 1

1. What ethnic group was largely responsible for building most of the early railways in the U.S. West?
2. What is the TV game show "Jeopardy" all about?
3. What language is spoken in Mexico?
4. What was the previous name of Sri Lanka?

Group 2

1. Name two countries that export tea.
2. What country makes panama hats? (not Panama!)
3. What is a twinkie and where can you buy one?
4. George W. Bush and his father, George H. W. Bush, were two father/son U.S. presidents. Who were the other two father/son presidents?

Group 3

1. Who was the first person to go into outer space, and where was he/she from?
2. Name two U.S. states that produce fresh oranges.
3. Where will the next two Summer Olympics be held and in what years?
4. Name two languages that are spoken in Lebanon.

Group 4

1. Where will the next Winter Olympics be held and in what year?
2. Who is Oprah Winfrey and what talents does she have?
3. Whose top selling album is titled *THRILLER*?
4. What does "She has a sweet tooth" mean?

Follow up ❀ *Write a short biography of **one** of the following:*

1. Oprah Winfrey
2. Michael Jackson
3. President John Adams
4. President George H. W. Bush

A Business That's Going to the Dogs

(CD 1 track 9) ♦ *[Full Text 148]*

Introduction ❀

Americans love their pets and treat them like members of the family. Recent statistics

show that Americans have more than 500 million pets. It's not surprising, therefore, to learn that pet-related businesses are popping up everywhere.

Americans are not alone in their love of animals. People in many countries of the world form strong emotional bonds with their pets. Pet worship is not a new cultural norm, either. Ancient Egyptians shaved off their eyebrows to mourn their pet cats that died.

Discussion ❀ *Talk about the photograph and read the caption under it. These dogs get picked up every morning and dropped off every night. Where do you think these dogs are going?*

With their seat belts secure, these passengers are set for the ride to the Common Dog, where they spend their days.

Dictation ❀ *Write the correct word or number in the blank space. Correct and discuss the dictation.*

The following interview is between dog day care owner and manager Richard Ross and a reporter.

Reporter: Richard, how did you get into the _____ _____ _____ business?

Richard: It all started when I agreed to _____ _____ _____ a neighbor's dog when she went on vacation for a week. She didn't want to put her dog _____ _____ _____ and since I have two dogs _____ _____ _____, I said sure. Then when a friend had to take a _____ _____ to Texas, he asked me to pet-sit his dogs. Then _____ _____ _____, and more and more working people who worried about their dogs getting lonely during the day started calling me up. _____ _____ _____ _____ _____, and here I am!

Reporter: So how many dogs do you have in your dog day care business now?

Richard: _____ _____; some days we have ten dogs, but we're licensed for _____.

Reporter: Do all of the dogs come for day care while their owners are _____ _____?

Richard: No, some come for _____ _____ _____ ____ _____ _____ _____ while the owners are on vacation. We have _____ _____ and _____ _____.

Reporter: _____ _____! What _____ _____ _____ do you charge?

Richard: If the owner _____ _____ his dog, we charge $28.00 a day. If they want

_____ – _____ _____ _____ in our van, the charge is higher,

about 35 _____.

Reporter: You provide transportation?

Richard: Yup. _____ pick up the dogs beginning at 7:30 a.m from their homes and

drop them off at 5:00 p.m. Dogs love _____ _____!

Reporter: Do you have any special _____ _____?

Richard: Well, they have to be _____, of course. And they must have

written proof of rabies and _____ _____. Once in a while

there's a dog that doesn't _____ _____ _____ other

dogs, but most love being here with their _____.

Reporter: I can see that you love your job.

Richard: You've _____ _____ _____ to do this. And now

that business _____ _____, I can hire more help!

Discussion 1 ❀ *Discuss these questions with a partner. Share your ideas with the class.*

Here is a questionnaire asked of thousands of Americans. Guess what percent of Americans pay special attention to their cats and dogs. Your teacher will give you the answers. What information surprised you?

Example: <u>49%</u> of dog owners prepare and cook special food for them.

_____ give their pets Christmas or birthday presents

_____ cook special food for their cats

_____ talk to their pets on the phone or answering machine

_____ call themselves the animal's mother or father

_____ sometimes dress up their pets for special occasions, such as Halloween

_____ sign letters or cards from themselves and their pets

_____ send their dogs to dog day care

Discussion 2 ❀

1. What pets are popular in your culture?

2. In your culture do:

> dogs live inside or outside the home?
>
> pets ever sleep with people?
>
> people cook special food for their pets?
>
> people have unusual pets such as monkeys, pigs, or crickets?
>
> people have animal hospitals and animal cemeteries?
>
> people have dog day care businesses?

3. Studies show that people's blood pressure drops when they talk to their pets. Think of some other advantages of having pets.

   • for children

   • for the elderly

   • for the handicapped

Follow up: Animal Idioms ❀

In the title of this unit, the expression "going to the dogs" is an idiom. Usually this expression means deteriorating or getting worse. Here are some other animal idioms. Find out what they mean.

1. She works like a dog.
2. He puts on the dog.
3. Let sleeping dogs lie.
4. He leads a dog's life.
5. They asked for a doggie bag at the restaurant.
6. We're in the dog days of summer.
7. She let the cat out of the bag.
8. I sent the letter by snail mail.

The Trials of Tipping

(CD 1 track 10) ♦ [Full Text 150]

Introduction ❀

Many international students and tourists are confused about the system of tipping when they come to the United States. The rules for tipping are very illogical and even Americans aren't always sure what kind of tip to leave. Let's say that your waitress was great, but your taxi driver was scary and your hair stylist was terrible. What do you do? Here is some help in figuring out the tipping dilemma.

Dictation ❀ *Write the correct word or number in the blank space. Correct and discuss the dictation.*

Tipping says "_____ _____" for good service, explains Judy Bowman,

president of Protocol Consultants International, who _____ _____ training

businesses and corporations in business and _____ _____. According

to Bowman, the _____ _____ _____ for tipping has gone up

in the last year, from _____ percent to _____ percent. "If you leave a

10 or 15% tip, you're going to get _____ _____."

The most important thing to remember about tipping is that you tip members of

the _____ _____ – people who rely on tips to make a living,

_____ _____ _____. Think about your waiter as the guy who sits

next to you in economics class and your _____ _____ may

change. Major tipping situations that people _____ _____ on a regular basis

include trips to the _____ _____, restaurants, taxis, _____, and food

delivery services. For each service, a basic tip is required, but it's _____ _____

_____ to decide how much to give. For someone who goes _____ and

_____ the call of duty, you would give a tip closer to the 20% range. For example,

when ordering a pizza, use the time as a _____ _____ _____.

If you're told the pizza will arrive in 20 minutes, but it comes in 15, you

_____ _____ _____. On the other hand, if the pizza is late or you've had

a _____ _____ dealing with the people in the _____ office, you are

_____ _____ to tip _____ or not at all. If you are not

going to tip, _____ _____. This way the delivery guy will know what he's done wrong. The same _____ _____ _____ should follow with taxi drivers, hairstylists, and waiters. But if you often go to the same hairstylist or restaurant and the service is good, tip well. The _____ _____ _____ _____!

Discussion ❀ *Discuss these questions with a partner. Share your ideas with the class.*

1. In the article above, the consultant recommends that if the service is bad, you should leave no tip. Another consultant may disagree with her. Why? What about taxi drivers and hair stylists – what would YOU do?

2. Would you complain if you think the service is bad? If so, would you complain to the server or to the management?

3. What are you looking for in service: informal friendliness? efficiency? formal correctness?

4. Have you ever seen "tip cups" in coffee shops and ice cream parlors asking for small change? You don't have to leave a tip. Can you explain why?

5. If you don't know whether or not to tip someone, what's the best thing to do?

6. According to the above article, Bowman says the tipping rate has gone up. Can you imagine a situation when the going rate might go down?

7. Can you explain why a waiter in a high-class restaurant makes more on tips than a waiter in a low-class restaurant – even though they both work equally hard?

Follow up ❀ *After you complete the two items below, share your answers with the class.*

1. What is the tipping custom in your culture? Is it a good system?

2. From the list, guess and check (√) the people Americans don't tip:

___ pizza delivery person

___ mail delivery person

___ package delivery person

___ newspaper delivery person

___ security guard

___ gas station attendant

___ airport luggage porter

____ flower delivery person

____ massage person

____ bartender

____ hotel porter

____ housepainter

____ mechanic

____ manicurist

Do You Believe in Ghosts?

(CD 1 TRACK 11) ♦ *[FULL TEXT 151]*

Introduction ❀

Do you think that ghosts exist? Do you know anyone who believes in ghosts? Before you do the dictation, talk about the different opinions people in your country have about ghosts.

Dictation ❀ *Write the correct word in the blank space. Correct and discuss the dictation.*

If you'd like to visit some places in the United States that have a reputation

_____ _____ _____ , you can buy the book, *The*

_____ _____ *of Haunted Places*, by Dennis Hauck,

a well-known _____ on paranormal phenomena. The book contains several

thousand _____ _____ places in countries around the world

and mentions many _____ _____ in the United States.

The most _____ _____ in the White House in Washington,

D.C., one that _____ _____ _____ by presidents and their families

on many occasions, is _____ _____ , the 16th president,

who _____ _____ in 1865. Lincoln had many tragedies_____

_____ _____ _____ , one of which was the death of his son,

Willie, at age 11. Lincoln believed _____ _____ _____ and

tried several times to _____ his son through seances in the White

House. Lincoln also had _____ of his own death and once told his

secretary that _____ _____ _____ was going to die in office and that he

could _____ his casket in the Rotunda Room of the White House.

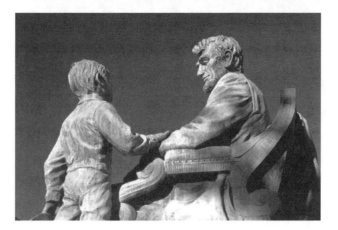

Abe Lincoln and his son Willie

Discussion 1 ❀ *Discuss these questions with a partner. Share your ideas with the class.*

1. Do you believe that some people have really seen ghosts?

2. Do you believe that a house can be haunted?

3. Do you know of any haunted places in your home city or country?

4. Do you believe that when people die, some part of them can stay with us?

5. If you have a good ghost story, tell it to the class!

Discussion 2 ❀ Psychics and Mediums

1. Zelda S. is a psychic who claims she can read people's auras and predict the future. She sometimes helps police find missing persons. She charges $15 for a 20-minute visit. She can also read tea leaves, read tarot cards, and read palms. Do you know anyone who has been to a psychic? Have you ever been to one?

2. Maureen H. is a certified licensed Asian bodywork therapist, stress management teacher, and spirit medium. In 1992 after a serious car accident left her with several broken facial bones and a fractured skull, Maureen credits a near miracle for her recovery. She feels she has been given a gift and has dedicated her life to giving hope and peace of mind to others. She charges $100 for a one-hour individual visit and is able to contact deceased family members and friends. Do you know anyone who has been to a spirit medium? Have you ever been to one?

3. If you wanted to find out more about mediums, what questions would you have for Maureen?

Follow up ❀ *Choose **one** of the following and write a paragraph.*

1. Go to Maureen's website, www.maureenhancock.com, and note the "frequently asked questions" section. What questions did you find the most interesting?

2. If you decide to go to a spirit medium, what kind of information would you like to learn?

Love Votes

(CD 1 track 12) ♦ [*Full Text 152*]

Introduction ❀

Here are some statements about dating and marriage. Notice the phrasal verbs that appear in this selection.

Dictation ❀ *After completing the dictation, vote* **YES** *if you agree with the statement, or* **NO** *if you disagree.*

Note: *the word "spouse" refers to a husband or wife. The word "mate" in this context means boyfriend or girlfriend.*

VOTE Yes or No
_____
_____
_____
_____
_____

1. You've _____ ____ _____ when someone you **really** like

   calls you _____ and _____ you _____ for the same night.

   You try to _____ _____ _____ the first date.

2. You _____ _____ that your spouse is infertile. You really want

   children of your own and cannot _____ _____.

   You leave your spouse.

3. Your favorite sister is _____ _____ marry a man

   who, in your opinion, is _____ _____. She is in love.

   You try to talk her _____ _____ _____.

4. You have a serious long-distance romance in your country. To relieve

   _____, you start a romantic _____ locally. You

   _____ ____ your commitment to the local person.

5. Your teenage daughter is dating a man of another _____. You try

   to get them to _____ _____ their relationship.

6. In order to _____ someone you love, you must _____

   _____ your _____ and change to theirs. You do it.

7. You give your mate a gift _____ $200; then you _____ _____

   a month _____. You ask _____ _____ _____.

8. You've been _____ _____ _____ a person who loves you

   much more than you love them. You've been _____ _____ about

   your feelings but your mate doesn't care. You end the _____

   now in order to _____ them a greater _____ later.

Discussion ❁ *Discuss these questions with a partner. Share your ideas with the class.*

1. Do you believe in love at first sight?
2. Would you consider using a computer or newspaper dating service?
3. Would you consider getting married and having only one child?

Follow up ❁ *Phrasal verbs are verbs with more than one word, such as* turn on *or* turn off.
Can you find the 12 phrasal verbs in this dictation?

Cheating in College

(CD 1 track 13) ♦ [*Full Text 153*]

Introduction ❦

Cheating has always been a problem in high schools and colleges. But now cheating has gotten so sophisticated and so widespread that it's raising serious questions about the integrity of young people and their education.

Dictation ❦ *Write the correct word or number in the blank space. Correct and discuss the dictation.*

1. Cheating in the classroom isn't just about _____ someone's paper or

   writing answers on a _____ _____. With the _____, cheating

   has gone _____ _____.

2. _____ of web sites offer _____ papers, class notes, and exams.

   Students may pay _____ _____ _____ for a research paper bought

   through the Internet.

3. _____ is the most common form of cheating, and university professors

   admit that it is _____ _____ _____. It depends _____ _____

   _____ of faculty members and a certain _____ _____

   _____.

4. More than _____ of 2000 students from _____ colleges nationwide

   _____ _____ _____ last year.

5. Experts say that most students cheat because of _____ _____.

6. _____ on college cheating shows that men and women _____

   admitted to _____ dishonesty; business and _____ majors

   were most likely to cheat, _____ _____ other majors.

7. Colleges are doing more _____ _____ cheating, and

   universities work with international students who come from _____

   that allow _____ another person's work _____

   _____ marks or footnotes.

8. At some schools, possible _____ _____ _____ includes

   _____, but most professors simply give the student an _____

   _____ _____ _____.

Discussion 1 ❀ *Discuss these questions with a partner. Share your ideas with the class.*

1. What forms of cheating are common in high schools or universities in your country?
2. Is it more common to find cheating in high schools or in universities?
3. Explain why it is wrong to cheat.
4. Why do students cheat?
5. If the teacher in your country catches someone cheating, what will happen?
   Will the student _____?
   - ♦ be given a 'zero' on the test
   - ♦ be kicked out of school
   - ♦ be given a warning
   - ♦ be physically punished
   - ♦ other?

Discussion 2 ❀ *Discuss these questions with a partner. Share your ideas with the class.*

How honest are <u>you</u>? Decide if the situation is definitely wrong, or if it is OK.

Example: You "cheat" on your boyfriend/girlfriend.   __*wrong*__

1. You tell your teacher you couldn't take the final exam because you
   were sick. In fact, you were not prepared for the exam because you
   didn't study all quarter. You ask to take a make-up exam.   _____

2. You ask a friend whose English is much better than yours to take the _____
   TOEFL test for you. You need a score of 250. You pay him $200.

3. You find a wallet with $200 in the school cafeteria. You
   keep it instead of reporting it to Lost and Found.   _____

4. You sell your eight-year-old car to an interested person. It needs
   new brakes and the cost of repair will be $900. You tell the buyer the
   car is in excellent condition.   _____

5. You are a waiter in a high-class restaurant and make excellent tips.
   When it's time to fill out your income tax form you report only
   70% of what you make.   _____

Follow up ❀ *Write a response to the teacher's aide.*

As a teacher's aide, I was helping proctor a placement exam for an ESL student who was taking a test to be placed in an ESL class. I discovered that during the exam he was mumbling. Then I saw headphones hidden under his hat. After that he began texting and I took his phone away. What do you think the school's policy should be regarding this incident?

Don't Be Fooled!

(CD 1 track 14) ♦ *[Full Text 154]*

Introduction ❀

Here are some tricky questions. Don't be fooled! But don't worry, you won't look foolish!

Dictation ❀ *After checking the dictation, try to figure out the answer with a partner.*

Example: Which is correct to say, "The yolk of an egg are white" or "The yolk of an egg is white?"   *Answer:* Neither. The yolk of an egg is yellow!

1. Mary Jones was born on December 27th, _____ her birthday is always _____ _____ _____. How can this be?

2. Frank was walking down Main Street when it started to _____. He did not have an umbrella and he wasn't wearing a hat. His clothes _____ _____, yet not a hair on his head _____ _____. How could this happen?

3. There is an _____ _____ still used in parts of the world today that _____ people to see through _____. What is it?

4. A taxi driver took a group of _____ to the train station. The station is _____ an hour away, but with terrible traffic, it took a full hour and _____ _____. On the return trip, the traffic was still as _____ and yet it took only _____ minutes. Why?

5. Do they have a 4th of July _____ _____?

6. Some months have _____ days; others have 31 days. How many have _____ days?

7. What five-letter word becomes _____ when you add _____ _____ to it?

8. A farmer had _____ _____. _____ _____ _____ died. How many did he have left?

9. A woman from New York _____ ten different men from that city, yet she didn't _____ _____ _____. None of the men _____ and she _____ _____. How was this possible?

10. Which one of the following words _____ _____ _____ with the _____ and why? Father, Aunt, Sister, _____, Mother, Uncle.

Riddles ❀

A
1. What is the longest word in the English language?
2. What has arms and legs but no head?
3. What never asks questions but gets many answers?
4. How many 46-cent stamps are there in a dozen?

B
a. a chair
b. a doorbell
c. twelve
d. smiles (because there's a mile between both s's)

What Used To Be

(CD 1 TRACK 15) ◆ *[FULL TEXT 156]*

Introduction ❀

When we talk about the present and how different it is today from the past, we usually use "used to."

Dictation Part A ❀

Fill in the blanks with the word or words you hear. Then, with a partner, check your dictation and find the answers to the incomplete sentences in Part B.

Example: Before electricity, people used to . . . read by candlelight.

1. Before _____, people used to . . .

2. The country that is now called _____ . . .

3. Before _____ _____, people used to. . .

4. _____ of years ago. . .

5. Before doctors became _____ , _____ used to. . .

6. In many _____ and not so ancient cultures, . . .

7. Before the car was _____, people used to . . .

8. The country that _____ _____ _____ called Ceylon . . .

9. People used to think that _____ . . .

10. Before _____, people used to . . .

Dictation Part B ❀

Use these phrases to complete the sentences in Part A above. There are two extra ones here! Then listen to Part B of the dictation, and check your answers against what you hear.

perform some operations	is now called Sri Lanka	travel by horse
were poisonous	people didn't use to travel by plane	read more
used to be called Siam	women never used to wear blue jeans	use typewriters
people used to have slaves	dinosaurs used to roam the earth	read by candlelight

Discussion ❀ *With a partner, talk about how to complete the sentences.*

1. I used to . . . but now. . .
2. My parents used to . . . but now. . .
3. People from my culture . . . but now . . .

Follow up ❀

Mary used to be poor, but she won $1,000,000 in the lottery. Her life has changed.
Write about how she used to live and what she does now.

Examples:

1. She used to drive a _____ but now she _____
2. She never used to _____ but now she _____

Facts About Drinking

(CD 1 TRACK 16) ♦ [FULL TEXT 157]

Introduction ❀

What is the legal drinking age in your state? Is underage drinking common in your community? Is drunk driving a problem where you come from? How much do you know about drinking? Talk about these questions and then try the dictation and decide if the statement is true or false.

Dictation ❀ *Write the correct word or number in the blank space. Correct and discuss the dictation.*

__ 1. Some people can drink a lot without _____ _____ drunk.

__ 2. Approximately 40% of _____ highway accidents are _____

_____.

__ 3. _____ _____ will make you drunker than staying with one

kind of alcohol.

__ 4. You can _____ _____ _____ with milk or food to slow down

the rate of intoxication.

__ 5. The best way to _____ _____ is to drink coffee and take a cold shower.

__ 6. _____ experts say that one out of every two Americans will

_____ _____ ____ a drunk driver.

__ 7. A person _____ _____ on alcohol.

__ 8. It is easy _____ _____ an alcoholic.

__ 9. Drinking during pregnancy can affect the _____ _____.

__ 10. Most alcoholics are _____ – _____ or older.

__ 11. Children of alcoholics are _____ _____ to develop alcoholism.

__ 12. _____ _____ is defined as five drinks _____ _____

_____ for men and _____ drinks within an hour for women.

__ 13. A _____ _____ is someone who drinks four to five drinks every night.

__ 14. All drinkers are _____ _____.

__ 15. _____ _____ account for 25% of the alcohol consumed in the U. S.

Discussion ❀ *Discuss these questions with a partner. Share your ideas with the class.*

Charles Dixon was arrested for drunk driving last year in Boston. No accident happened but this was the second time the police had stopped him. His license was taken away for six months; he was fined $1000 and ordered to attend an alcohol-education program. Do you think this punishment was fair? Why or why not?

What kind of punishment should these people get?

A. a warning   B. go to jail – how long?   C. pay a fine – how much?

D. take away the license – how long?   E. attend an alcohol-education program

1. A woman was driving drunk. She was speeding and driving recklessly. No accident happened and this was her first offense. She was 19 years old.

2. A man, age 50, was driving drunk and hit another car. The people in that car were not seriously injured but had to go to the hospital by ambulance for examination.

3. A drunk woman, age 22, hit another car. The person in the other car died.

Follow up ❀ *The attitude toward drinking is different in every country. Write a paragraph about the attitude toward drinking in your culture.*

Nutrition Quiz

(CD 1 TRACK 17) ♦ *[FULL TEXT 160]*

Introduction ❀

How much do you know about your general health and nutrition? Here are some statements that may surprise you!

Dictation ❀

First, listen and write the words you hear in the blank spaces. Then, work with a partner and decide if the statement is true or false. Discuss your answers with the class.

__ 1. Low-fat milk has more _____ _____ _____ milk.

__ 2. Multivitamin pills can give you _____ _____.

__ 3. It's better to eat a _____ _____ and a smaller dinner.

__ 4. People who do not eat meat, fish, or chicken are _____ ____ _____ _____ those who do.

__ 5. Fresh vegetables are always _____ _____ _____ frozen.

__ 6. If you want to make one _____ in your diet, it is better to eat three balanced meals a day, _____ _____ on _____.

__ 7. A glass or two of wine _____ _____ will help you sleep well.

__ 8. _____ helps keep you in good _____.

__ 9. When you're _____ __ _____, it's better to drink white wine _____ ____.

__ 10. You've been asked to _____ _____ _____. A good serving size would be _____ _____ _____ ____ a deck of cards.

__ 11. Butter contains _____ _____ _____ _____.

__ 12. Women who eat at least _____ servings of fruits and vegetables _____ reduce their _____ of diabetes by _____.

Discussion ❀ *Discuss these questions with a partner. Share your ideas with the class.*

1. How does the diet of your country compare with the American diet?
2. Has the diet of the people in your country changed in the past 10 or 20 years?

Follow up ❀ *Write about a typical weekday breakfast, lunch, and dinner in your family.*

How's Your Mental Health?

(CD 1 TRACK 18) ♦ *[FULL TEXT 162]*

Introduction ❀

Mental health issues affect large numbers of people, not only in the United States but all over the world. Years ago, mental illness was not discussed in public, as if it were a deep, dark, shameful secret to be kept only within the family. Nowadays, with more information and research about different mental illnesses, people can educate themselves about the nature of these illnesses and learn how to get the right kind of help for themselves, a family member, or friend, when it is needed.

Dictation ❀ *Write the correct word or number in the blank space. Correct and discuss the dictation.*

The Surgeon General of the United States recently _____ that _____ in _____ Americans suffers from a _____ illness. Although some may feel this is overstated, imagine that:

♦ _____ in _____ women will experience _____ depression in their lives, as will _____ in _____ men.

♦ Eight to twelve percent of the population experiences a significant _____ _____.

♦ _____ in _____ children has attention deficit hyperactivity disorder (ADHD).

♦ One percent of the population has _____ depression or bipolar illness.

♦ _____ percent of the population has schizophrenia.

Through education and information it is important to be able to look at depression, anxiety, ADHD, and sleep _____ not as _____ but rather as real and medically based illnesses. Considering mental health problems to be _____ – _____ based means that far too many will go unrecognized and _____.

The _____ _____ mental illness is depression. Different

forms of depression _____ from short-term, low mood after a

_____ life experience to an _____ form of depression linked to

decreased energy, interest, and _____ along with changes in appetite

and sleep – called _____ _____.

Depression may also take place in women following _____ as well as

in people during certain _____ of the year. Being unable to perform

at work, having little wish to _____, and becoming _____

from family members may all take place during depression. Depression very much

needs to be viewed as a _____ illness and not as a weakness. Recognizing

and treating depression not only _____ life but also _____ lives.

Discussion ❦ *Discuss these questions with a partner. Share your ideas with the class.*

1. Low-mood depression is steadily increasing among students. In some schools there is a 40% increase in the need for counseling sessions. Here are a few reasons why. Which do you think are the most serious? Can you think of any other reasons?

   - fitting in
   - academic pressure/meeting expectations
   - finding a career
   - adjusting to a new place/homesickness
   - fear of war/bio-terrorism
   - financial woes
   - sexual orientation

   - forming relationships
   - information overload
   - long-term abuse
   - problems at home (family/economic)
   - bereavement
   - your reasons

2. More serious forms of depression are often treated with medication, once the diagnosis has been made. Prozac and other anti-depressant drugs are commonly used and allow sufferers to live a fairly "normal" life. What other mental illnesses mentioned in the dictation do you think would most likely require medication? Why?

3. Universities, especially those with high suicide rates, have been forced to make a major overhaul of their mental health services. Here are some changes that are taking place throughout the United States. In small groups or with the class, discuss these changes and add your own ideas.

   - extended appointment hours to see a psychotherapist; some have walk-in service
   - 100% medical insurance coverage for off-campus services
   - creation of education and outreach programs aimed at making students more comfortable in seeking help
   - support groups for those coming out as gays and lesbians and for minority students
   - your idea

Follow up ❦

To learn more about mental illness, you can log on to a number of web sites. One you can begin with is the interactive web site "Ask PsychMD" at: www.askpsychmd.com/index.htm. To search for other sites, type in "mental illness" or a specific disorder such as bipolar disorder and find one that will give you the information you want. Here are a few suggestions:

- Sleep Disorders
- Childhood Depression
- Postpartum Depression – an illness a woman can get after giving birth
- Anxiety Disorder

Alternative Medicine

(CD 1 TRACK 19) ♦ [FULL TEXT 163]

Introduction ❀

In 1976, when President Richard Nixon established diplomatic relations with the People's Republic of China, Americans learned about acupuncture, which the Chinese had been practicing for centuries. Since then and into the twenty-first century Americans have become increasingly interested in acupuncture and other forms of "alternative medicine."

Dictation ❀ *Write the correct word or number in each blank space. Correct and discuss the dictation.*

_____ _____ _____, the idea of treating pain with acupuncture or hypnosis would have _____ _____ _____ _____ within the medical mainstream. _____ _____ _____ _____ _____ _____ _____ are offering patients alternative or complementary therapies _____ _____ _____ _____.

A big reason for the trend _____ _____ _____. A Harvard study reported _____ _____ _____ _____ _____ _____ to alternative practitioners _____ _____ _____ _____ _____ to primary care doctors, spending $27 billion (a good part of it _____ _____ _____) on alternative treatments.

Proponents say complementary techniques, particularly mind-body therapies, _____ _____ _____. They are non-invasive and have _____ _____ _____. And they tap into the healing power of the mind.

Discussion ❀ *Discuss these questions with a partner. Share your ideas with the class.*

- Is alternative medicine popular in your country?
- Have you or anyone in your family tried alternative medicine? What did you try and what were the results?

Follow up ❀ *Research **one** of the following and report back to the class.*

herbal medicine	hypnosis	acupuncture	biofeedback
massage therapy	meditation	chiropractics	

Chinese New Year

(CD 1 TRACK 20) ♦ *[FULL TEXT 164]*

Introduction ❀

New Year's Eve and New Year's Day are major holidays in all cultures because there is a universal hope that one can begin anew. Because of different lunar and solar calendars, the holidays are celebrated at different times of the year and in different ways. The one thing that is not different is that there are special symbolic foods for the New Year whenever it is celebrated. Americans toast the New Year with champagne. Jews dip apples or bread in honey hoping for a sweet year. The Chinese, too, have many symbolic foods.

Dictation ❀ *Write the correct word or number in each blank space. Correct and discuss the dictation.*

In feudal times, the Chinese believed that the eve of the New Year marked the Kitchen God's departure to heaven _____ _____ _____

_____ _____ _____ _____. To welcome the Kitchen God _____ _____ _____ _____ in the New Year, each family feasted and performed a "spring-cleaning." The spring festival symbolized _____ _____ _____ and the earth's seasonal return to life.

"We serve _____ _____ that are auspicious for the New Year," Danny Woo, the manager at the Jumbo Seafood Restaurant in _____, says. He is planning an _____ – _____ _____ _____, because eight in Chinese _____ _____ _____ _____, since it sounds like the word "_____."

_____ _____ _____ are cooked only in their whole form to represent a year _____ _____ _____ _____

_____.

One traditional Chinese _____ for the New Year is Clams in Black Bean _____, because their _____ resemble Chinese coins, which

_____ _____. Another _____ recipe is Good Luck Dumplings.

Discussion ❋ *Discuss these questions with a partner. Share your ideas with the class.*

♦ What special or symbolic foods does your family prepare for your New Year or any other important holiday?

♦ Why is feasting or fasting connected to certain holidays?

♦ Lin Yutan, a Chinese philosopher, said, "What is patriotism but the love of good food we ate in our childhood?" What do you think it means?

♦ Chinese restaurants can be found in many countries besides China. What other ethnic restaurants are there in your country?

♦ Following is the recipe for "Good Luck Dumplings." Read over the recipe with your partner, making sure that you both understand the vocabulary and what to do. Perhaps some students in the class can try making them.

Good Luck Dumplings

Ingredients

1 lb pork, beef, or tofu *(drained of excess liquid)*

¼ tsp salt

1 clove minced garlic

1 tsp minced fresh ginger root

¼ tsp pepper

2 tbsp sesame oil

1 cup chopped green onions

1-2 packages of wonton wrappers

vegetables of your choice *(make sure they are blanched and drained of excess liquid)*

Directions

1. In a large bowl combine all dumpling ingredients except wonton wrappers, and mix thoroughly.
2. Wrap about 1 ½ tbsp of filling in each wrapper. With fingers, lightly wet edges of wrapper with water. Firmly pinch edges.
3. Place dumplings in lightly salted water and cook gently for about 10 minutes. Drain; then run cold water over cooked dumplings to avoid sticking.
4. Add dumplings to boiling chicken broth and cook until done.
5. Add green onions for garnish.

Follow up ❋ *Choose **one** of the following*

♦ Gather favorite recipes from members of the class. Compile them and give everyone a copy.

♦ Write about a favorite family holiday meal, your memories about eating it, and what it means to you.

Independence Day

(CD 1 track 21) ◆ *[Full Text 165]*

Introduction ❀

Until the twentieth century, wars took place mainly in summer, and the War of Independence was no exception. This was partly because most roads were just dirt tracks that turned to deep mud in winter, stopping armies from traveling easily. Armies had to travel at a time of year when there would be plenty of food in the fields to feed the men. Independence Day in the United States is celebrated in July and is the most important patriotic holiday of the year.

Dictation 1 ❀ *There are two columns below, listing the names of countries and their dates of independence. Fill in the blank spaces with the date you hear. With a partner, match the country to the date.*

1. France	a. July 4, 1776
2. United States of America	b. _____
3. Brazil	c. _____
4. Australia	d. _____
5. Canada	e. _____

Discussion ❀ *Discuss these questions with a partner. Share your ideas with the class.*

1. One of the dates above is very different from the others. Why?
2. Does your country have a day when it celebrates its independence? How is it celebrated?

Dictation 2 ❀ *Write the correct word or number in each blank space. Correct and discuss the dictation.*

In this dictation you will hear about some of the ways the U.S. celebrates its birthday. _____ _____, the anniversary of the day the Declaration of Independence was signed, is a day in the United States _____ _____ _____ _____ _____. About a week before the celebration, you will see small and large flags flying, and stores beginning to display _____, _____, and _____ _____.

In almost every little town across the country, there is a parade. People line the route _____ _____ _____ _____ _____. The parade often begins with a line of _____ _____ dating from the nineteen twenties and thirties, followed by _____ _____ marching and playing patriotic songs like *Yankee Doodle Dandy*. Even _____

_____ _____ _____ dazzling technology, Americans like to _____

_____ _____ of an old-fashioned parade.

In the afternoon, friends and family will gather for a _____

_____ barbecue. At one time, fresh salmon and fresh peas were part of

a _____ _____, but the _____

lends itself to chicken, steaks, and hot dogs, _____ – _____

_____ _____.

Everyone waits for dark, _____ _____

_____ _____. Most large cities have extravagant concerts and

firework displays. In Boston, on the Esplanade by the Charles River,

_____ _____ _____ will gather to watch and hear

the Boston Pops. Some of the crowd _____ _____ _____

_____ at 6:00 A.M. to get good seats for this great show. The crowd will

_____ _____ to the well-known songs, and a popular star will read

the Declaration of Independence while _____ _____

_____ in the background. The last piece, Tchaikovsky's *1812 Overture*,

will include real cannons firing. This is the traditional ending, and the crowd cheers

as the orchestra plays _____ _____ _____. Finally the moment arrives,

and you can hear the crowd's oohs and aahs as the sensational half-hour of

fireworks _____ _____ _____ _____ _____ _____ with red, white,

and blue shells that burst _____ _____ _____ _____

_____ _____ _____.

Discussion ❀ *Discuss these questions with a partner. Share your ideas with the class.*

1. If you celebrate an independence day in your country, how do you celebrate it?
2. Do you think patriotism is a good thing?

Follow up ❀ *Choose **one** of the following. Do some research, and write or talk about what you find.*

◆ Describe how your country celebrates an important religious or patriotic holiday.
◆ Did your country fight for its independence from another country? Write or talk about the history of your country's independence.
◆ Are there countries or groups within countries trying to gain independence today?

Natural Disasters

(CD 1 TRACK 22) ♦ [FULL TEXT 166]

Introduction ❋

Natural disasters such as earthquakes, floods, droughts, tsunamis, volcanoes, hurricanes, epidemics, and cyclones happen almost every day somewhere in the world. Some of these disasters are very small, and no one is hurt. Others are much more serious and cause death and destruction. Here is a chart of some world disasters that have happened in the past 90 years.

Dictation ❋ *Listen to the information about each natural disaster and write what you hear in the correct box. Check your information with a partner before telling the class.*

Disaster	Country	Continent	Year	Killed
epidemic	Nigeria			
	Colombia	South America		
			2005	1,836
Tsunami				
	China		1931	
drought		Asia		
				143,000
	Bangladesh			

Discussion ❋ *Work with a partner and share your information.*

1. Can you guess what the epidemic was in Nigeria? Did it happen in other countries?
2. What other volcanic eruptions do you know about? Where are they?
3. What causes tsunamis? What other countries were affected by the 2004 tsunami?
4. Japan is the country with the most earthquakes. What other countries get them?
5. Hurricanes in the U.S. do not kill as many people today as in the past. What is the reason for that?
6. Why was the disaster in Bangladesh so deadly?

Follow up ❋ *Write about a natural disaster that you know about. Then read it to the class.*

Scary Movies

(CD 1 TRACK 23) ♦ [FULL TEXT 167]

Introduction ❀

Everyone everywhere enjoys movies. Whether we see a movie in a theater, rent a video to watch at home, or watch a movie on TV or our computer, we are transported out of our own lives into other worlds. Surprisingly, one of the most popular movie genres is horror. Why do you think people enjoy horror movies?

Dictation ❀ *Fill in the blank spaces with the words you hear. With a partner, check your responses.*

Why would anyone voluntarily _____ _____ _____ a _____ – _____ _____ filled with _____, _____, and _____? Why would anyone pay _____ _____ _____? How could it be _____?

Theories about _____ _____ tell us that humans try to pursue _____ and _____ _____. _____, psychologists give _____ _____ for why we enjoy _____ _____ _____.

The first is that the person is not _____ _____ of the movie but excited by it. _____ _____ is that viewers are willing to endure the terror _____ _____ _____ enjoy the very happy _____ ____ _____ at the end.

Some of the scariest movies in English of all time are *Psycho* (_____), *The Shining* (_____), and *The Silence of the Lambs* (_____), as well as series like *Halloween* and *Halloween II*.

Discussion ❀ *With a partner, discuss these questions.*

1. Do you like horror movies? Why? What is your favorite horror movie?
2. What is your favorite movie genre? (romantic comedy, action, etc.)
3. Do you have some favorite movies? What are they?
4. Do you have some favorite actors and actresses? Who are they?
5. Do you watch movies in English? With or without subtitles? Has this helped you learn English?

Follow up ❀ *Choose **one** of the following.*

1. Take a poll and report your findings to the class. These are some questions you might start with. Be sure to add at least two of your own.

   How many movies do you watch in a month?

   Do you prefer to watch movies in a movie theater or at home?

   Do you watch English-language movies with or without subtitles?

2. Write about **one** of the following.
   ◆ A Movie I Remember From My Childhood
   ◆ My Favorite Movie
   ◆ Advice to an English Language Learner About How To Watch a Movie in English

3. Check the movie pages in your local paper. What movies are playing? Read the ads. List the movies and beside each try to write what movie genre it is. (For example, *Friday the 13th* – horror, *The Sound of Music* – musical)

Family Reunion

(CD 1 TRACK 24) ◆ [FULL TEXT 168]

Introduction ❀

America is a very mobile society. Children and grandchildren may live hundreds or even thousands of miles away from their parents and grandparents. Because of this the Clarks have a summer family reunion every year. It is an occasion for picnics, barbecues, and other kinds of fun. This year all of the Clarks' sons, wives, and grandchildren are coming.

Dictation ❀ *Write the correct word or number in each blank space. Correct and discuss the dictation.*

After doing this dictation, solve this logic puzzle. Put together the name of each husband and wife and how many children they have, where they came from, and when they arrived.

The Clarks were _____ _____ _____ June 20th, when their

_____ sons, and their sons' wives and children, were coming to their Utah home

for a _____ _____. Everyone was _____ to arrive by _____

_____. Each couple had _____, _____, or _____ children. From

the following clues, can you match the sons with their wives, determine how many

children each couple had, _____ their time of _____, and _____

_____ where each family lived?

1. One couple _____ no state or national borders in _____ _____ the homecoming.

2. The couples _____ _____ _____ at _____, _____, _____, _____, _____, and _____.

3. The couples from _____ and _____ _____ the same number of children.

4. George _____ only one child, a boy. Eileen has only two girls, and Carol _____ only one girl.

5. The son from _____ _____ at _____.

6. Pat, who hails from Wyoming, _____ three children and did not arrive either first or last.

7. Frank _____ _____ from _____ and _____ after _____, two hours after his brother from Japan.

8. Bert and Bob don't _____ the same number of children. The son from Texas _____ one _____ child than the son from Wyoming. The son from Arizona _____ one more child than Frank.

9. Wendy _____ after Jill, who _____ after Linda. But Linda _____ before Eileen, who _____ before _____.

10. Keith _____ all night and _____ before _____ with his three hungry children.

11. Bert _____ his wife and two children into the car that morning and _____ three hours after Frank.

Discussion ✤ *Discuss these questions with a partner. Share your ideas with the class.*

1. Do you like this kind of logic puzzle? If you were able to solve it, share it with your partner or the class.
2. On what important occasions does your entire family get together? Are you a small family or a large family?
3. What do you think are the advantages of families living near each other? Are there any disadvantages?

Follow up ✤ *Do **one** of the following.*

♦ Find a logic puzzle (or another kind of puzzle) for your partner or the class to do.
♦ Write about a reunion that you have experienced. (family, school)

Tall, Taller, Tallest

(CD 2 TRACK 1) ♦ *[FULL TEXT 169]*

Introduction ❀

Were you the shortest person in your elementary school class? The tallest? How much did you weigh at birth? Do you think that size plays any part in who you are?

1 inch = 2.54 centimeters
1 foot = 12 inches = 0.348 meters
1 pound = 16 ounces = 0.454 kilograms

Pair Dictation ❀ *Student A*

Work in pairs and dictate to each other. Student A has half of the dictation and reads their lines to Student B, who has the other half. A dictates and B writes; then Student B dictates and A writes, until the dictation is complete. With your partner, correct the dictation.

We are growing taller. In the _____ _____

_____ growth has been dramatic. _____ _____

Norwegian soldiers averaged _____ _____ _____.

American soldiers _____ _____ _____ _____

___ averaged five feet tall _____ _____ _____.

Today the average Californian male is _____ _____

_____ _____ and weighs 188 pounds.

In the Netherlands, _____ _____ _____

_____ _____ in the world, the average

height of men _____ _____ ____ _____

_____ _____.

The difference between _____ _____ _____ may disappear

some day. _____ _____ _____ _____ men were 30%

taller _____ _____. Today height differences _____ _____ .

Pair Dictation ❀ *Student B*

Work in pairs and dictate to each other. Student A has half of the dictation and reads their lines to Student B, who has the other half. A dictates and B writes; then Student B dictates and A writes, until the dictation is complete. With your partner, correct the dictation.

_____ _____ _____ _____. ____ _____ last 200

years _____ _____ _____ _____. In 1760

_____ _____ _____ five foot three.

_____ _____ drafted in World War 1 _____

_____ _____ _____ and 140 pounds. _____

_____ _____ _____ _____ _____ 5 feet 10 ½

inches _____ _____ _____ _____ .

_____ _____ _____, home to the tallest population

_____ _____ _____, _____ _____ _____ ____

_____ is nearly 6 feet 1 inch.

_____ _____ _____ men and women _____

_____ _____ _____. Thousands of years ago _____ _____

_____ _____ than women. _____ _____

_____ average 7%.

Discussion ❀ *Work with a partner and answer these questions. Share your responses with the class.*

♦ Discuss the advantages and disadvantages of being tall or short.
♦ If you're a woman, are you taller than your mother? If you're a man, are you taller than your father?
♦ Have you ever wished you were taller or shorter?
♦ (*for a man*) Would it matter to you if your wife were much taller than you?
(*for a woman*) Would it matter to you if you were much taller than your husband?

Follow up ❀ *Choose one of the following.*

1. Do some research on increasing birth size. Present what you've learned to the class.
2. Do some research on changing sizes of men and women in another country. Present what you've learned to the class.
3. Because the U.S. is not on the metric system, people from other countries have some problems when they first arrive in the U.S. Write about your experience with pounds, ounces, feet, inches, *etc.*

Cloning

(CD 2 TRACK 2) ♦ *[FULL TEXT 169]*

Introduction ❀

Genetic research has resulted in, and is resulting in, some of the most important medical breakthroughs in many years. Scientists can study and possibly find solutions to genetic diseases for which there have been no previous cures. On the other hand it has also resulted in controversy since cloning can now produce a copy of an animal. The world was first amazed in 1997 when scientists in Scotland announced the birth of the world's first successfully cloned mammal, Dolly the sheep.

Pair Dictation ❀ *Student A*

Work in pairs and dictate to each other. Student A has half of the dictation and reads their lines to Student B, who has the other half. A dictates and B writes; then Student dictates and A writes, until the dictation is complete. Then with a partner, correct the dictation. In the following pair dictation, after a Texas researcher announced that he had cloned a cat, a newspaper reporter has asked two people what they think about it.

Nicole has two cats _____ _____ _____ _____. But she'd never want to _____ ____ _____ with either one of them.

"____ _____ _____ ___ _____. I'm not for it at all," _____ _____-_____-_____ _____ when asked her opinion _____ ____ _____ cloning a cat.

"_____ _____ _____ _____ human cloning, _____ ____ _____ _____. It's one more step. _____, _____ _____ _____," she said in answer _____ _____ _____ _____.

She said that _____ _____ _____ even if it meant _____ _____ for Picky and Tornado, _____ _____ _____.

"I love them to death, _____ _____ _____ _____ _____."

Jim, a 33-year-old man, said, "_____ _____ _____. Cats shouldn't be cloned. _____ _____ _____ _____. They're spending _____ _____ _____ _____ when they could be spending it _____ _____ _____ _____ _____: find a cure _____ _____ ____ _____." Jim has a fox terrier _____ _____. "I love Max. _____ _____ _____ _____ and I don't know _____ ___ _____ _____ if he died today. _____ _____ _____ _____ _____ _____, it's up. _____, _____ _____."

Pair Dictation ❀ *Student B*

Work in pairs and dictate to each other. Student A has half of the dictation and reads their lines to Student B, who has the other half. A dictates and B writes; then Student B dictates and A writes, until the dictation is complete. Then with a partner, correct the dictation. In the following pair dictation, after a Texas researcher announced that he had cloned a cat, a newspaper reporter has asked two people what they think about it.

_____ _____ _____ _____ and treasures them both. _____

_____ _____ _____ _____ double the pleasure _____ _____

_____ ____ _____.

   "I'm not one for cloning. _____ _____ _____ _____ _____ _____ " the

23-year-old said _____ _____ _____ _____ about a researcher

_____ _____ _____.

   "It will lead to _____ _____ and that is wrong.

_____ _____ _____ _____. Sheep, and now this," _____

_____ _____ _____ to a reporter's question.

_____ _____ _____ cloning was wrong _____ _____

_____ _____ getting duplicates _____ _____ _____ _____,

her two cats. " _____ _____ _____ ____ _____, but I

wouldn't clone them."

   _____, ____ ____-_____-_____ _____, _____, " Leave life alone.

_____ _____ ____ _____. Nobody should be cloned. _____

_____ way too much money _____ _____ _____ _____

_____ _____ on research for something useful: _____ _____

_____ for AIDS or cancer." _____ _____ ____ _____

_____ named Max. "_____ _____ _____. He's 12 years old _____

_____ _____ _____ what I would do _____ _____ _____

_____. But when his time is up, _____ _____. Unfortunately, that's life."

Discussion ❀ *Discuss the following questions with your partner. Share your ideas with the class.*

If you had a pet that you loved dearly and it was going to die soon, would you clone it if you had the opportunity? Why or why not?

Follow up ❀

- ◆ Do some research to find out what good things have occurred as a result of stem cell research. Present your information to the class.
- ◆ Make up some questions about cloning. Ask several people to answer your questions Present your results to the class.

Older Learners

(CD 2 track 3) ♦ *[Full Text 170]*

Introduction ❀

In many countries people are living longer, and they have opportunities that they didn't have when they were working. Retirement is not only a time to relax, but also a time to complete some unfinished challenges. Going back to school was an unfinished challenge for Chi-Hing, who tells her story in the following dictation.

Pair Dictation ❀ *Student A*

In the following dictation Student A will read their lines to Student B, who has the other half of the paragraph. (Student A dictates and Student B writes.) Then Student B dictates and Student A writes, until the paragraph is complete. When you are finished, check what you have written with your partner.

    For Chi-Hing _____ _____ _____ _____than education. That's why _____ _____ _____ she decided _____ _____ _____ _____ _____ to get her high school diploma. _____ ____ _____ ___ ___ _____ Chi-Hing put on a cap and gown _____ _____ ___ _____ _____ _____ _____ in a ceremony on the eve of the _____ _____ _____.

    "It had always been my dream _____ _____ _____ _____ _____," said Chi-Hing. "_____ _____ _____ _____ _____ _____, you can learn. _____ _____ _____ _____ _____."

    Chi-Hing moved to Boston _____ _____ ____ _____. While she had been a teacher _____ _____ _____ _____, she did not speak English, _____ _____ _____ _____ the credentials _____ _____ _____ _____ _____. So she went to work _____ ____ _____ _____ _____ and concentrated on _____ _____ ____ ____ _____.

    She also took _____ _____ _____ ____ _____ _____. When a broken hip _____ _____ ____ _____, she saw an opportunity. She had plenty of free time _____ _____ _____ were grown. _____ _____ _____ that she was too old _____ _____ _____ _____ _____.

    She met a college professor ____ _____ ____ to finish her education. "___ _____ _____ _____ _____," Chi Hing recalled. "___ _____ _____ I wanted to learn, _____ _____ _____ _____ _____. He encouraged me; _____ _____ _____ _____ _____ _____ _____. And I did."

Pair Dictation ❀ *Student B*

> *In the following dictation Student A will read their lines to Student B, who will have the other half of the paragraph. (Student A dictates and student B writes.) Then Student B dictates and Student A writes, until the paragraph is complete. When you are finished, check what you have written with your partner.*

_____ _____ nothing was more important _____ _____.
_____ _____ at age 68 _____ _____ to go back to school _____
_____ _____ _____ _____ _____. After a year and a half
_____ _____ _____ ____ _____ _____ _____ and received a
Boston Public School Diploma _____ _____ _____ _____ _____
_____ _____ _____ Chinese New Year.
    "_____ _____ _____ _____ _____ _____ to go back to school,"
_____ _____. "No matter what age you are, _____ _____ _____.
It is never too late."
    _____ _____ _____ _____ from China in 1975. _____
_____ _____ _____ ____ _____ in China and Okinawa, _____ _____
_____ _____ _____ , nor did she have _____ _____
to teach in the U.S. _____ _____ _____ ____ _____ in a day care center
_____ _____ _____ taking care of her family. _____ _____
_____ Adult Education classes and English classes.
    _____ _____ _____ _____ forced her to retire _____ _____
_____ _____ _____. _____ _____ _____ _____
_____ _____ and her children _____ _____. But
she worried _____ _____ _____ _____ _____ to go back to school.
    _____ _____ _____ _____ _____ who encouraged
her _____ _____ _____ _____. "He could speak nine languages,"
_____ _____. "I told him _____ _____ ____ _____,
but I was too old. _____ _____ ____; he told me I could do it. _____
____ _____."

Discussion ❀ *Discuss these questions with a partner. Share your ideas with the class.*

1. What do you think are some of the problems that Chi-Hing had going back to school at the age of 68?
2. Chi-Hing was an inspiration to many of the younger students in her class. Have you ever met or read about someone much older than you who has done something that has inspired you?
3. In the United States some older people are going back to college – for example, veterans returning from the military. What do you think are the advantages and disadvantages for a college student of having older students in the class? What do you think are the advantages and disadvantages for the older student?

Follow up ❀ *Write about **one** of the following.*

♦ Pretend you are 65 and recently retired. What are some of the things you would like to do?
♦ Did you grow up with a grandmother or a grandfather? Describe them and tell how they spent their older years.

Food as a Second Language ♦ A Recipe

(CD 2 TRACK 4) ♦ *[FULL TEXT 171]*

Introduction

One of the nice things about living in a country with immigrants from many different countries is the variety of food that we can prepare. Whether you come from Italy, China, Somalia, Mexico, or Turkey, food is a common bond and a way we share our heritage. Here is a recipe for banana bread that is easy to make and has many variations. You choose whether you would have this for breakfast, for lunch, or with afternoon tea.

Pair Dictation ❀ *Student A*

Work in pairs and dictate to each other. Student A has half of the dictation and reads their lines to Student B, who has the other half. A dictates and B writes; then Student B dictates and A writes, until the dictation is complete.

Banana Bread
Ingredients

2 ripe bananas, mashed

_____ _____

¾ cup of flour

_____ _____ _____ _____ _____ _____

1 teaspoon of baking soda and _____ _____ ___ _____ _____

½ teaspoon of vanilla

_____ _____ ____ _____

3 tablespoons of skim milk

_____ _____ _____ _____, _____

2/3 cup of coconut flakes (____ _____ _____)

Directions

Put _____ _____ ____ _____ with 2 eggs, baking soda,

_____ _____ _____. Stir and add all other

ingredients. _____ _____ _____ _____ ____ _____ inch pan

and bake at _____ _____ _____ _____ _____.

Pair Dictation ❀ *Student B*

Work in pairs and dictate to each other. Student A has half of the dictation and reads their lines to Student B, who has the other half. A dictates and B writes; then Student B dictates and A writes, until the dictation is complete.

Banana Bread
Ingredients

____ _____ _____, _____

2 eggs

_____ _____ _____ _____

½ cup oil or melted margarine

___ _____ ___ _____ _____ ____ ½ teaspoon of baking powder

_____ _____ ____ _____

¾ cup of sugar

____ _____ _____ _____ _____

2/3 cup of walnuts, chopped

_____ _____ ____ _____ _____ (or chocolate chips)

Directions

_____ bananas in a bowl _____ _____ _____, _____ _____,
and baking powder. _____ _____ _____ _____ _____
_____. Put in an 8 by 8 _____ _____ _____ _____ _____
350 degrees for 60 minutes.

Discussion ❀ *With two other classmates, create a menu for your new International Restaurant. Include three appetizers or soups, three main dishes, and three salads or desserts.*

Follow up ❀ *Write out a popular recipe from your culture and share it with the class. Or find a recipe on Epicurious.com and share it with the class.*

Hanging Out to Dry

(CD 2 TRACK 5) ♦ *[FULL TEXT 172]*

Introduction ❀

Sixty million people in three hundred thousand private communities across the United States are forbidden to dry their laundry anywhere outside, even in their backyards. The communities say that clothes hanging outside on clotheslines are an eyesore, a sign of poverty, and would lower property values. A few states have passed laws allowing anyone in the state to hang laundry outdoors, and people in other states are fighting for this right. The "right-to-dry" movement has been growing.

Pair Dictation ❀ *Student A*

*In this dictation work in pairs and take turns dictating to each other. Student A has half of the dictation and reads their words, phrases or sentence to Student B, who has the other half. (A dictates and B writes.) Then student B reads their words, phrases, or sentence, and Student A writes. Continue until the sentences are complete. When you are finished, compare what you have written with your partner and decide if each sentence is **For (F)** hanging clothes out to dry or **Against (A)** hanging clothes out to dry.*

__ 1. Clotheslines _____ _____ _____ to fight climate change _____

_____ _____ _____ instead of electricity.

__ 2. It indicates _____ if you put out _____ _____.

__ 3. People have _____ _____ from their windows that they'd like to keep.

__ 4. _____ ____ _____ _____ is a waste of energy.

__ 5. I think _____ dangling _____ _____ _____ are beautiful

if they're _____ the environment.

__ 6. _____ _____ _____ _____ when I look out my window

_____ _____ _____ birds, trees, and flowers, _____ _____.

__ 7. _____ _____ account for _____ _____ _____ _____ electricity

_____ by U.S. households.

__ 8. _____ _____ _____ saves money, _____ _____ last longer

_____ _____ _____, conserves energy, _____ _____

_____ _____.

Pair Dictation ❀ *Student B*

In this dictation work in pairs and take turns dictating to each other. Student A has half of the dictation and reads their words, phrase, or sentence to Student B, who has the other half. (A dictates and B writes.) Then Student B reads their words, phrase, or sentence, and Student A writes. Continue until the sentences are complete. When you are finished, compare what you have written with your partner and decide if each sentence is For (F) hanging clothes out to dry or Against (A) hanging clothes out to dry.

__ 1. _____ are one way _____ _____ _____ _____

using sun and wind _____ _____ _____.

__ 2. _____ _____ poverty _____ _____ _____

_____ your wash.

__ 3. _____ _____ nice views _____ _____ _____ _____

_____ _____ _____ _____.

__ 4. Using a clothes dryer _____ _____ _____ _____ _____.

__ 5. _____ _____ sheets _____ in the wind _____ _____

_____ _____ helping _____ _____.

__ 6. These rules are why _____ _____ _____ _____ _____

_____ I now see _____, _____, _____ _____,

not laundry.

__ 7. Clothes dryers _____ _____ 6% of the total _____

consumed _____ _____ _____.

__ 8. Giving up dryers _____ _____, helps clothes _____

_____ and smell better, _____ _____, and

promotes physical fitness.

Discussion ❀ *Discuss the following questions with a partner. Then share your ideas with the class.*

1. Do you use a dryer or hang your clothes out to dry?
2. Do you think that people should have the right to hang their laundry out to dry?
3. In your community or in your country do people hang out their laundry?
4. Are you concerned about global warming? What do you do to save energy?
5. "This has become an issue because it concerns individual rights, private property, social class, aesthetics, and the environment." What does the speaker of this quotation mean by this statement?

Follow up ❀ *Choose one of the following.*

♦ Research or think of simple ways people can save energy. Write about your ideas or do a short presentation for the class.
♦ What is one of the ways your community or your country is trying to save energy? Write about this or do a short presentation.

Three Little Words

(CD 2 TRACK 6) ♦ *[FULL TEXT 173]*

Introduction ❀

From the time we are very small until we are adults, our parents give us advice. The late humorist Erma Bombeck, in a funny column called *Three Little Words*, said, "When you think about it, we've all raised our kids using a minimum of three exclamatory sentences: No! Don't! and Stop! Used unsparingly, they can take a parent through 20 or 30 years of living."

Pair Dictation ❀ *Student A*

In this dictation work in pairs and dictate to each other. Student A has half of the paragraph and reads their lines to Student B, who has the other half. (A dictates and B writes.) Then Student B dictates and A writes, until the paragraphs are complete. When you are finished, check what you have written with your partner.

_____ _____ until you've done _____ _____.

No dessert _____ _____ _____ _____ your plate.

_____ _____ because you're not going. _____ _____.

No dishes, _____ _____. No time for _____ _____?

No more arguing _____ _____ _____.

    Just when you think _____ _____ _____ _____

_____ to say "No," _____ _____ "_____." Don't

screw up. _____ _____ _____ _____.

Don't _____ _____ _____ _____, do as I say. _____

_____ _____ _____ thank you. _____ _____

_____ what I'm saying? _____ _____ _____ say it again.

_____ _____ _____ there is nothing _____

"_____!" _____ _____. Stop driving me crazy. _____ _____

that creep. _____ _____ like you're _____ _____ _____. Stop

trying to be _____ _____ _____. Stop being _____ _____.

    They're all familiar. We couldn't have survived without them. But wouldn't it be sad if No! Don't! and Stop! were the only things they learned from us ... and those three little words shaped their lives?

Pair Dictation ❀ *Student B*

In this dictation work in pairs and dictate to each other. Student A has half of the paragraph and reads their lines to Student B, who has the other half. (A dictates and B writes.) Then Student B dictates and A writes, until the paragraphs are complete. When you are finished, check what you have written with your partner.

No television _____ _____ _____ your homework.

_____ _____ until you've cleaned up _____ _____.

No hurry _____ _____ _____ _____. No way.

_____ _____, no movie. _____ _____ _____ your mother?

_____ _____ _____ with your brother.

_____ _____ _____ _____ there are no more ways

_____ _____ "_____," along comes "Don't." _____ _____

_____. Don't forget your sweater. _____ do as I do, _____ _____

_____ _____. Don't forget to say _____ _____. Don't you hear

_____ _____ _____? Don't make me _____ _____

_____.

For sheer drama _____ _____ _____ like "Stop!"

Stop humming. _____ _____ _____ _____. Stop dating

_____ _____. Stop acting _____ _____ a big shot.

_____ _____ _____ _____ something you're not.

_____ _____ so negative.

They're all familiar. We couldn't have survived without them. But wouldn't it be sad if No! Don't! and Stop! were the only things they learned from us ... and those three little words shaped their lives?

Discussion ❀ *Discuss these questions with a partner. Share your ideas with the class.*

- ♦ What advice did your parents give you when you were younger?
- ♦ What advice do your parents give you now?
- ♦ If you're a parent, what advice do you give to your children?
- ♦ Can you think of advice that you've been given that you didn't take?

Follow up ❀ *Choose **one** of the following to write about.*

- ♦ Write to a friend who is beginning to study English and give the friend advice.
- ♦ Write to a 16-year-old who wants to quit high school. Give this teenager advice.
- ♦ Write to a friend who wants to move to a new country. Give the friend advice.

What's So Funny?

(CD 2 TRACK 7) ♦ *[FULL TEXT 173]*

Introduction ❀

There are many kinds of jokes and everyone likes to hear a good one. But what is a good joke? One that makes you laugh! Humor is different from culture to culture, and what is funny in one culture may not be funny in another. Here are two jokes for you to rate according to your personal taste. If you don't understand the humor, you say, "I don't get it." The punchline of a joke is the final sentence that causes you to laugh.

Pair Dictation ❀ *Student A*

Student A will have half of the joke and will read their lines to Student B, who has the other half. Student A dictates and Student B writes; then Student B dictates and A writes, until the joke is complete. When you are finished, decide if the joke is funny or not.

Is the joke: a. pretty good   b. not that good   c. not funny at all

Joke 1

A person who _____ _____ _____ is bilingual.

____ _____ _____ speaks three languages _____ _____.

A person who _____ _____ languages is _____.

What is ____ _____ _____ speaks one language? ____ _____.

Joke 2

An English teacher _____ _____ _____ on the board:

"_____ _____ _____ _____ is nothing."

The teacher _____ _____ the students to _____

_____ _____ _____.

The men wrote: "_____, _____ _____ _____, is nothing."

The women wrote: "_____! Without her, _____ _____ _____."

Pair Dictation ❈ *Student B*

Student A will have half of the joke and will read their lines to Student B, who has the other half. Student A dictates and Student B writes; then Student B dictates and A writes, until the joke is complete. When you are finished, decide if the joke is funny or not.

Is the joke: a. pretty good   b. not that good   c. not funny at all

Joke 1

_____ _____ _____ speaks two languages _____ _____.

A person who _____ _____ _____ is trilingual.

___ _____ _____ speaks four _____ ___ multilingual.

_____ ____ a person who _____ _____ _____?

An American.

Joke 2

_____ _____ _____ wrote these words ____ _____ _____:

"woman without her man _____ _____" _____ _____

then asked _____ _____ _____ punctuate the words correctly.

_____ _____ _____: "Woman, without her man, ____ _____."

_____ _____ _____: "Woman! _____ _____, man is nothing."

Follow up ❈ *Find a joke. Turn it into a dictation. Make copies and read it to the class.*

Who Would Say That?

(CD 2 track 8) ♦ *[Full Text 174]*

Introduction ❀

Sometimes you overhear a conversation and guess what people are talking about. In this dictation, guess who's talking.

Pair Dictation ❀ *Student A*

Work in pairs and dictate to each other. Student A has half of the dictation and reads their lines to Student B, who has the other half. A dictates and B writes; then Student B dictates and A writes until the dictation is complete. Write your guess on the line indicated.

Example: "It's a beautiful top floor two-bedroom."   **Who?**   *real estate agent*

1. "It's a 2009 and _____ _____ _____ with

   only _____ _____." _____

2. "Do you have any _____ _____? " _____

3. "We expect _____ _____ _____ _____ in ten minutes." _____

4. " ____ _____ _____ _____ should go on a diet." _____

5. "Would you like ____ _____ _____ _____ this

   time? A perm? ____ ____ _____?" _____

6. "I predict that _____ _____ _____ meet the perfect

   man and _____ _____." _____

7. "_____ ____ _____ _____ for Reggie. Now it's _____ three

   to three." _____

8. "May I see your _____ _____ _____

   registration please?" _____

9. "Open _____." _____

10. "The fine is _____ _____ ____ _____ for each one

    that is _____." _____

Pair Dictation ❀ *Student B*

Work in pairs and dictate to each other. Student A has half of the dictation and reads their lines to Student B, who has the other half. A dictates and B writes; then Student B dictates and A writes, until the dictation is complete. Write your guess on the line indicated.

Example: "It's a beautiful top floor two-bedroom."   Who?   *real estate agent*

1. "_____ ____ _____ _____ in perfect condition _____

   _____50,000 miles."   _____

2. "____ _____ _____ _____ spare change?"   _____

3. "_____ _____ to be taking off ____ _____ _____."   _____

4. "I think that Snoopy _____ _____ _____ ____ _____."   _____

5. "_____ _____ _____to try something different, _____

   _____? ___ _____? Or a frost?"   _____

6. "____ _____ _____ next year you'll _____ _____

   _____ _____ _____ get married."   _____

7. "It's a home run _____ _____. _____ _____ tied _____

   ____ _____."   _____

8. "_____ ____ _____ _____ driver's license

   and _____ _____?"   _____

9. "_____ wide."   _____

10. "_____ _____ _____ 10 cents a day ____ _____

    _____ _____ _____ overdue."   _____

Discussion ❧ *With a partner, add quotation marks to the story,* **The Hare and the Tortoise**. *Share your responses with the class.*

One day a hare was bragging about how fast he could run. I have never been beaten, he said. When I put forth my full speed, I challenge anyone here to race with me.

The tortoise said quietly, I accept your challenge.

That is a good joke, said the hare. I could dance around you all the way.

Keep your boasting until I've been beaten, answered the tortoise. Shall we race?

A race! What fun, said the hare.

So a course was fixed, and a starting line was made. The race began and the hare, being such a swift runner, soon left the tortoise far behind. About halfway through the course, the hare said Oh my, I have plenty of time to beat that slow tortoise. I'll take a nap. Meanwhile, the tortoise never for a moment stopped, but went on with a slow but steady pace straight to the end of the course.

When the hare awoke from his nap, he thought it was time to get going. And off he went faster than a speeding bullet, but it was too late. He dashed up to the finish line where he met the tortoise, who was patiently awaiting his arrival. What took you so long, the tortoise asked.

The moral of this story is: **"Slow and steady wins the race."**

Follow up ❧ *Here are some other morals from famous fables. Explain their meanings.*

1. One man's meat is another man's poison.
2. Don't count your chickens before they're hatched.
3. Beauty is only skin deep.
4. Live and let live.
5. Clothes do not make the man.
6. Every man for himself.
7. Look before you leap.
8. Necessity is the mother of invention.

Limericks and Tongue Twisters

(CD 2 TRACK 9) ◆ [FULL TEXT 176]

Introduction

Limericks are silly poems with five lines that are told in a particular rhyming pattern: AABBA. Listen to the rhythm as your teacher reads this example. Then practice saying it aloud with the class.

There once was an odd man named Rod	(A)
Who loved his old car more than God,	(A)
So much that he said	(B)
To his wife, "When I'm dead,	(B)
Bury me in my car on Cape Cod."	(A)

Pair Dictation ❀ *Student A*

Student A will have half of a limerick and will read her/his lines to Student B, who has the other half. Student A dictates and Student B writes; then Student B dictates and A writes, until the limerick is complete. When you are finished, practice reciting the limericks.

1. There once was an old man from Nesser

    _____ _____ _____ _____ ____ _____.

    It at last grew so small,

    _____ _____ _____ _____ _____,

    And now he's a college professor!

2. _____ ____ ___ _____ _____ _____ ____

    Who loved to go fishing for squid.

    ____ _____ _____ _____ ____ _____

    Who was very defiant,

    ____ _____ _____ _____ ___, _____ ____ ____. (_____ _____.)

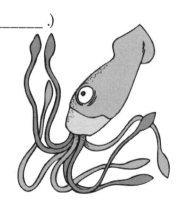

Pair Dictation ❀ *Student B*

Student A will have half of a limerick and will read her/his lines to Student B, who has the other half. Student A dictates and Student B writes; then Student B dictates and A writes, until the limerick is complete. When you are finished, practice reciting the limericks.

1. _____ _____ _____ _____ _____ _____ _____ _____

   Whose knowledge grew lesser and lesser.

   _____ _____ _____ _____ _____ _____,

   He knew nothing at all,

   _____ _____ _____ _____ _____ _____!

2. There was a young fellow named Sid

   _____ _____ _____ _____ _____ _____ _____.

   But he caught quite a giant

   _____ _____ _____ _____,

   And ate Sid all up, yes it did. (Poor kid.)

Tongue Twisters ❀

Tongue twisters force you to twist your tongue. Tongue twisters must be said fast — the faster the better. Most tongue twisters need to be repeated a certain number of times. Listen to your teacher and repeat. Then try these with a partner.

- ◆ Chet chewed two chewy cherries.
- ◆ Frank's frying five fresh fish.
- ◆ Eight apes ate Amy's grapes.
- ◆ Bella built a beautiful brick building.
- ◆ Donna's dogs dig deep ditches.
- ◆ Little Ilene lied a lot.

Follow up ❀ *Fill in the blank with a word that seems to fit. Share your tongue twister with the class.*

1. A big black bug bit a big black bear on his big black _____.
2. Six slippery snails slid _____ seaward.
3. Silly Sammy slurps _____'s soup.
4. Betty beat a bit of butter to make the batter _____.
5. Ollie and Annie's anniversary is in _____.

The New World Language

(CD 2 TRACK 10) ♦ [FULL TEXT 177]

Introduction ❀

As a language with many origins -- Romance, Germanic, Norse, Celtic, and so on – English is a very messy language. It is also very elastic. New words enter it daily. Nouns become verbs before we know it. It is a language that is always changing, and that increases the difficulties for people who are studying it as a second language.

Pair Dictation ❀ *Student A*

In this dictation work in pairs and take turns dictating to each other. Student A has half of the dictation and reads their words, phrases or sentence to Student B, who has the other half. (A dictates and B writes.) Then Student B reads their words, phrases, or sentence and Student A writes. Continue until the dictation is complete. When you are finished, compare what you have written with your partner.

English is _____. Some 380 million people _____ _____ as their

first language, _____ _____ another 250 million people _____ _____ as their

second language. _____ _____ _____ _____ _____. By 2050 _____

_____ _____ that half of the world _____ _____ _____ ____

_____ proficient in it. _____ _____ _____ _____ of

globalization, _____ _____ _____, politics, and diplomacy.

_____ _____? Not because English is easy. _____, _____

_____ _____. But the verbs _____ _____ _____ irregular, _____

_____ _____, and the match between _____ _____

_____ a nightmare.

Pair Dictation ❀ *Student B*

In this dictation work in pairs and take turns dictating to each other. Student A has half of the dictation and reads their words, phrases, or sentence to Student B, who has the other half. (A dictates and B writes.) Then Student B reads their words, phrases, or sentence and Student A writes. Continue until the dictation is complete. When you are finished, compare what you have written with your partner.

_____ _____ everywhere. _____ _____ _____ _____

speak it _____ _____ _____ _____, and perhaps

_____ _____ _____ _____ speak it _____ _____

_____ _____. A billion are learning it. _____ _____

it is predicted _____ _____ ____ ____ _____ will be more or less

_____ _____ _____. English is the language _____

_____, of international business, _____, _____

_____.

How come? _____ _____ _____ ____ _____. Sure,

genders are simple. _____ _____ _____ tend to be _____,

the grammar bizarre, _____ _____ _____ _____ spelling and

pronunciation _____ _____.

Discussion ❀ *With a partner, decide whether you agree or disagree with these statements. Discuss why.*
- ◆ English is an easy language to learn.
- ◆ English is an easier language to learn than my first language.
- ◆ American English is very different from British English.
- ◆ There are many similarities between English and my first language.

Follow up ❀ *Write about **one** of the following topics.*
1. My best experience speaking English
2. My worst experience speaking English
3. Some of the problems I've encountered studying English

All About Weather

(CD 2 TRACK 11) ♦ [FULL TEXT 178]

Introduction

If you live in an area where weather is constantly changing, weather is probably one of the topics that people speak about all the time, both to strangers and to friends. In many areas, the three main topics of conversation are politics, sports, and the weather. This is not so unusual, since weather plays a major role in our daily lives.

Pair Dictation ❀ *Student A*

Student A will have half of the weather jokes and will read their part to student B, who has the other half. Student A dictates, and student B writes; then Student B dictates, and Student A writes, until each joke is finished. With your partner, correct the dictation and decide which joke you think is funnier.

Joke 1

I had just moved north _____ _____ _____ _____ about the severity of the winters. My anxious questions _____ _____ _____ brought this reply from a native. "_____, _____ _____ _____ _____ _____: early winter, _____, late winter, _____ _____ _____."

Joke 2

The Michaels family owned _____ _____ _____ _____ _____ just yards away from _____ _____ _____ _____. Their land had been the subject _____ _____ _____ _____ between Canada and the United States _____ _____. Mrs. Michaels, _____ _____ _____ _____ _____ _____ _____, lived on the farm _____ _____ _____ _____ _____ _____. One day, her son came into her room _____ _____ _____. "I just got some news, Mom," _____ _____. "_____ _____ has come to an agreement _____ _____ _____ _____ _____. They've decided that our land _____ _____ _____ _____ _____ _____ _____. We have the right to approve or disapprove _____ _____ _____. What do you think?"

"_____ _____ _____ _____ ?" _____ _____ _____.

"Jump at it! _____ _____ _____ _____ and tell them we accept. _____ _____ _____ _____ _____ _____ another one of those Canadian winters."

Pair Dictation ❀ *Student B*

Student A will have half of the weather jokes and will read their part to student B, who has the other half. Student A dictates, and student B writes; then Student B dictates, and Student A writes, until each joke is finished. With your partner, correct the dictation and decide which joke you think is funnier.

Joke 1

_____ _____ _____ _____ _____ and was feeling apprehensive _____ _____ _____ _____ _____ _____. _____ _____ _____ about the weather _____ _____ _____ _____ _____ _____. "Ma'am, we have four seasons here: _____ _____, midwinter, _____ _____, and next winter."

Joke 2

_____ _____ _____ _____ a small farm in Canada _____ _____ _____ the North Dakota border. _____ _____ _____ _____ of a minor dispute _____ _____ _____ _____ _____ _____ for generations. _____ _____, who had just celebrated her ninetieth birthday, _____ _____ _____ _____ with her son and three grandchildren. _____ _____, _____ _____ _____ _____ _____ _____ holding a letter. "_____ _____ _____ _____ _____, _____," he said. "The government _____ _____ _____ _____ _____ with the people in Washington. _____ _____ _____ _____ _____ is really part of the United States. _____ _____ _____ _____ _____ _____ _____ _____ of the agreement. _____ _____ _____ _____?"

"What do I think?" his mother said. "_____ _____ _____! Call them right now _____ _____ _____ _____ _____. I don't think I could stand _____ _____ _____ _____ _____ _____."

Discussion ❀ *Discuss these questions with a partner. Share your ideas with the class.*

♦ What is the climate like in another country that you have lived in?

♦ Which climate would you prefer to live in, one that has four seasons -- summer, autumn, winter, and spring -- or one that is pleasantly warm and sunny 365 days a year?

♦ How does climate affect the economy? What are the economic advantages and disadvantages of living in a warm or cold climate?

♦ What is the worst weather you have ever experienced?

♦ How does weather affect your mood?

Cooperative Learning ❀ Working with Idioms

Find the meaning of the following idioms. Work in four groups of three or four. Using the Internet or asking native speakers, each student finds out about one or more items listed below and reports back to the group. Then all four groups present what they have learned.

Group 1

1. Break the ice.
2. Shoot the breeze.
3. It's the tip of the iceberg.
4. He was three sheets to the wind.

Group 2

5. It's raining cats and dogs.
6. I'll take a rain check.
7. Don't rain on my parade.
8. I can weather the storm.

Group 3

9. I'm under the weather.
10. It was a real snow job.
11. I was thunderstruck.
12. The idea came out of the blue.

Group 4

13. I was snowed under with work.
14. She gave me the cold shoulder.
15. She was on cloud nine.
16. Her head was in the clouds.

Are you Superstitious?

(CD 2 track 12) ♦ [Full Text 180]

Introduction ❀

A superstition is an illogical belief that some action will affect something that is unrelated to the action. For example, many people believe that breaking a mirror will result in seven years of bad luck. They also believe that knocking on wood will insure good luck to continue. They carry good-luck charms with them to keep themselves safe. Many people will say that they are definitely not superstitious. Their behavior, however, will show that they occasionally are. What about you? Are you superstitious?

Pair Dictation ❀ *Student A*

In the following dictation you will work in pairs and dictate to each other. Student A will have half of the paragraph and will read their lines to Student B, who has the other half. (Student A dictates and Student B writes.) Then student B dictates and A writes, until the paragraph is complete. When you are finished, check what you have written with your partner.

A young Japanese woman _____ _____ was being wheeled _____

_____ _____ _____ when she noticed the number over the door. ____

_____ _____ _____ softly. _____ _____ _____

_____ and asked what was wrong. _____ _____ _____, but

explained that the Japanese character _____ _____ _____ _____ is pronounced

the same_____ _____ _____ _____ _____ _____ "_____."

Already concerned about her health, _____ _____ _____ to be wheeled

_____ _____ _____ _____ "_____." Although she said _____

_____ _____ _____ _____ _____, Keiko was unable

_____ _____ _____ _____ _____ _____.

The surgery went well despite the room number, _____ _____ _____

_____ _____ _____. Had the hospital personnel _____

_____ _____that she was being scheduled _____ _____ _____, her feelings

might have become known _____ _____ _____ _____

_____ _____ into a different room. _____ _____ _____,

_____ _____, would have been appropriate_____ "_____"

_____ _____ _____ also means "life."

Pair Dictation ❀ *Student B*

In the following dictation you will work in pairs and dictate to each other. Student A will have half of the paragraph and will read their lines to Student B, who has the other half. (Student A dictates and B writes. Then Student B dictates and A writes, until the paragraph is complete. When you are finished, check what you have written with your partner.

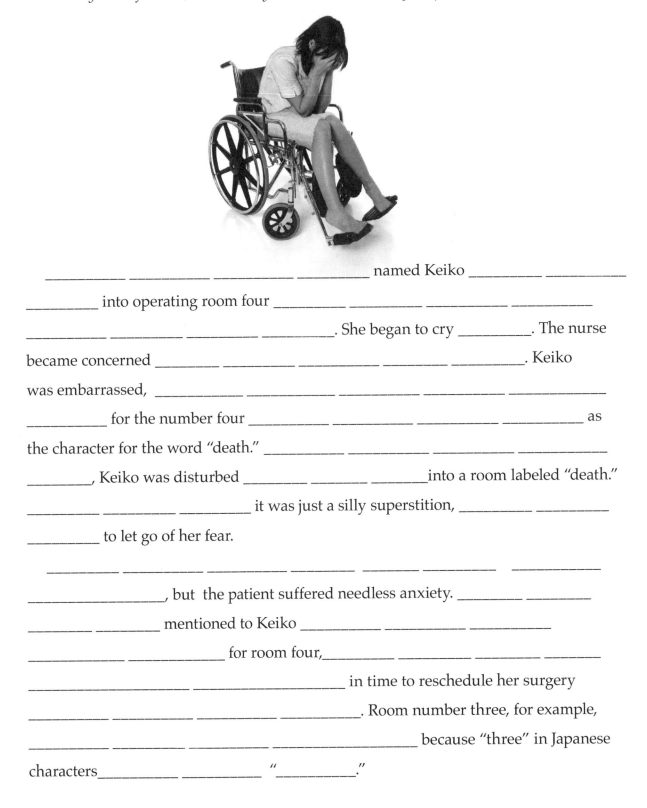

_____ _____ _____ _____ named Keiko _____ _____

_____ into operating room four _____ _____ _____ _____

_____ _____ _____ _____. She began to cry _____. The nurse

became concerned _____ _____ _____ _____ _____. Keiko

was embarrassed, _____ _____ _____ _____ _____

_____ for the number four _____ _____ _____ _____ as

the character for the word "death." _____ _____ _____ _____

_____, Keiko was disturbed _____ _____ _____ into a room labeled "death."

_____ _____ _____ it was just a silly superstition, _____ _____

_____ to let go of her fear.

_____ _____ _____ _____ _____ _____ _____

_____, but the patient suffered needless anxiety. _____ _____

_____ _____ mentioned to Keiko _____ _____ _____

_____ _____ for room four, _____ _____ _____ _____

_____ _____ in time to reschedule her surgery

_____ _____ _____ _____. Room number three, for example,

_____ _____ _____ _____ because "three" in Japanese

characters _____ _____ "_____."

Discussion ❀ *Discuss these questions with your partner. Share your ideas with the class.*

1. Do you believe in some superstitions?

2. Do you practice any superstitions? Why?

3. In the pair dictation, the numbers three and four both had some meaning. Are there numbers in your culture that are either lucky or unlucky? What are they? Do you know why they're lucky or unlucky? Can you understand how Keiko felt?

4. Athletes often have lucky clothing or lucky jewelry that they wear when they're playing, because they connect these items with victory. Do you have a lucky number, a lucky color, a lucky piece of clothing, or a lucky piece of jewelry?

5. Here are some common superstitions; are you familiar with any of them?

   a. Placing a bed so that it faces south and north brings misfortune.

   b. If you blow out all the candles on your birthday cake with the first puff, you will get your wish.

   c. If your cheeks suddenly feel on fire, someone is talking about you.

   d. It's bad luck to cut your fingernails at night.

   e. If the palm of your right hand itches, it means you will soon get money.

   f. Never open up an umbrella in your house. It will bring bad luck.

   g. Never have thirteen people around a dinner table, because one will die.

6. Share a superstition from your culture.

Follow up ❀ *Write about **one** of the following.*

1. In your culture, what do people think causes bad luck?

2. Where do people learn about superstitions? Think back to your childhood and write about where you learned about good luck and bad luck.

3. Why are you not superstitious?

All About Ice Cream

(CD 2 TRACK 13) ♦ *[FULL TEXT 181]*

Introduction ❀

"I scream. You scream. We all scream for ice cream." Whether it's *gelato* (Italy) or *crème glacé* (France), ice cream is one of the most popular desserts in almost every country in the world.

Directions ❀

Work with a partner and read the sentences which are about the history of ice cream. Put them in logical or chronological order. You may have to do a little research to connect some of the events to a date.

_____ The developing of ice harvesting in the 19th century led to Nancy Johnson's invention of the hand-cranked ice cream freezer.

_____ In the 1st century Nero sent messengers to the mountains to collect snow so that he could make ices with fruit and honey.

_____ The ice cream cone became popular at the World's Fair in 1904.

_____ During the Prohibition era many people ate ice cream instead of drinking alcohol, and breweries were often converted into ice cream factories.

_____ Marco Polo introduced Europe to a frozen milk dessert that he had enjoyed in the Far East.

_____ Before the development of modern refrigeration in the first few decades of the twentieth century, ice cream was a luxury reserved for special occasions.

_____ Catherine de Medici went to France in 1533 as the bride of Henri II with recipes for frozen desserts.

_____ By 1970 there were over 500 flavors.

_____ Americans named this dessert "ice cream" instead of "iced cream" in the mid-1700s.

Pair Dictation ❀ *Student A*

Work in pairs and dictate to each other. Student A has half of the dictation and reads their lines to Student B, who has the other half. A dictates and B writes; then Student B dictates and A writes, until the dictation is complete. With your partner, check the dictation.

1. Americans consume _____ _____ _____ than any other country _____ _____ _____ on a per capita basis. The Australians _____ _____ _____. In 1924, _____ _____ _____ ate eight pints a year. _____ _____ that figure had jumped _____ _____ _____ _____ _____.

2. _____ is the most popular flavor _____ _____ _____, getting anywhere _____ _____ _____ _____ of sales. _____ comes in _____ _____ _____ with about _____ _____ _____ of the market.

3. One out of every five _____ _____ _____ share their treat _____ _____ dog or cat.

4. One of the _____ _____ in ice cream _____ _____. Without it, _____ _____ would be as hard _____ _____ _____. Some types _____ _____ _____ are more than _____ _____.

5. _____ _____ _____ _____ _____ of ice cream _____ _____ are avocado, garlic, azuki bean, jalapeno, and dill pickle.

6. A major invention _____ _____ _____ _____ _____ was the ice cream sundae. _____ _____ _____ comes from Sunday, but no one knows why. _____ _____ _____ _____ _____ was made in _____ _____ in 1988 _____ _____ nearly _____ _____.

Pair Dictation ❀ *Student B*

Work in pairs and dictate to each other. Student A has half of the dictation and reads their lines to Student B, who has the other half. A dictates and B writes; then B dictates and A writes, until the dictation is complete. With your partner, check the dictation.

1. _____ _____ more ice cream _____ _____ _____

    _____ in the world _____ _____ _____ _____

    _____. _____ _____ come in second. _____ _____, the

    average American _____ _____ _____ ___ _____. By 1997

    _____ _____ _____ _____ to 48 pints a year.

2. Vanilla _____ _____ _____ _____ _____ in the U.S.A.,

    _____ _____ from 20 to 29% ____ _____. Chocolate

    _____ _____ a distant second _____ _____ 9 to 10% ____

    _____ _____.

3. _____ _____ ____ _____ _____ ice cream eaters _____ _____

    _____ with their _____ ___ _____.

4. _____ ____ _____ major ingredients ____ _____ _____ is air.

    _____ _____, the stuff _____ ____ _____ _____ as a

    rock. _____ _____ of ice cream _____ _____ _____

    75% air.

5. Among the most unusual flavors ____ _____ _____ ever manufactured ____

    _____, _____, _____ _____, _____, _____

    _____ _____.

6. _____ _____ _____ in the late 19th century _____ _____ _____

    _____ _____. Its odd name _____ _____ _____,

    _____ _____ _____ _____ _____. The biggest ice cream

    sundae _____ _____ _____ Alberta, Canada, ____ _____

    and weighed _____ 55,000 pounds.

Discussion ❦ *With a partner, discuss the following questions.*

♦ Is ice cream one of your favorite foods?

♦ Is ice cream popular in your country? Is there something special about the ice cream in your country? How is it different from ice cream in another country you have lived in or visited?

♦ What is your favorite flavor? Your favorite brand?

♦ Where is ice cream sold in your country? (on the street, from an ice cream truck, in an ice cream store, in the supermarket)

♦ Do people in your country eat ice cream while walking on the street?

Follow up ❦ *Choose* **one** *of the following.*

♦ What associations or memories do you have with ice cream? (an ice cream truck selling ice cream outside your school, your grandmother feeding you ice cream, at a hot beach) Write about one of your ice cream memories.

♦ Create a poll. Make up five or more questions to ask five to ten people. Report what you learned to the class.

♦ There are various alternatives to regular ice cream for people with special diets. (ice cream made from soy milk) Do some research and tell the class what you learned or write a short report.

♦ Ice cream shows up in early Persian and Chinese history. Do some research about the very early history of ice cream and either write a short report or tell the class what you learned.

♦ Write a short poem about ice cream.

Childhood

(CD 2 TRACK 14) ♦ *[FULL TEXT 182]*

Introduction

Humans have the longest childhood. In developed countries we can generally say that childhood lasts for approximately eighteen years. For many people it is a time of endless play, free from many responsibilities. It is also usually a time for learning, but not working. Unfortunately this is not true for many children in the world.

Pair Dictation ❊ *Student A*

Work in pairs and take turns dictating to each other. Student A has half of the dictation and reads their words, phrase, or sentence to Student B, who has the other half. (A dictates and B writes.) Then Student B reads their words, phrase, or sentence and Student A writes. Continue until the dictation is complete. When you are finished, compare what you have written with your partner.

An estimated _____ _____ _____ ages five to fourteen

_____ _____ _____ _____ _____. This is one in six children

_____ _____ _____.

Millions of _____ work in dangerous situations. _____

_____ _____ _____, work with chemicals and pesticides _____

_____, and work with dangerous machinery. _____

_____ _____ a four-year-old _____ _____ _____ _____

_____ to keep the child _____ _____ _____.

Millions of _____ _____ _____ work as

domestic servants _____ _____ where they are

_____ _____ _____. Of course, _____

_____ _____ _____ from going to school.

_____, _____ _____, some as young as ten, _____

_____ _____ and are fighting _____ _____

around the world.

Pair Dictation ❀ *Student B*

Work in pairs and take turns dictating to each other. Student A has half of the dictation and reads their words, phrase, or sentence to Student B, who has the other half. (A dictates and B writes.) Then Student B reads their words, phrase, or sentence and Student A writes. Continue until the dictation is complete. When you are finished, compare what you have written with your partner.

_____ _____ 158 million children _____ _____

_____ _____ are engaged in child labor. _____ _____

_____ _____ _____ _____ in the world.

_____ _____ children _____ _____

_____ _____. They work in mines, _____

_____ _____ _____ _____ in agriculture,

_____ _____ _____ _____ _____. One

example is _____ _____-_____-_____ tied to a rug loom _____

_____ _____ _____ from running away.

_____ _____ very young girls _____ _____

_____ _____ in households _____

_____ _____ exploited and abused. _____ _____, work

prevents these children _____ _____ _____ _____.

Also, many children, _____ _____ _____ _____ _____ are

child soldiers _____ _____ _____ in wars _____

_____ _____.

Discussion ❀ *Discuss the following questions with your partner.*

1. Is this information surprising to you? Why or why not?
2. Are there many children who are working and not going to school in your country?
3. Are there any children who are soldiers in your country?
4. As a child or a teenager did you ever work (full-time, part-time)? What were the advantages and disadvantages?

Follow up ❀ *Choose **one** of the following.*

♦ Find out what organizations are fighting against child labor and what they are doing.
♦ Find out where children are fighting in wars at this time.
♦ Write about work that you did before you were eighteen. (at home, part-time job, full-time job)

Bono

(CD 2 TRACK 15) ♦ *[FULL TEXT 183]*

Introduction ❀

Bono (Paul David Hewson) is known internationally as a rock star who writes and performs political and personal songs. He is a philanthropist who organizes and participates in events that raise a lot of money to fight hunger and poverty and make the world a better place.

Work with a partner and read the sentences, which outline a short biography of Bono. Put them in chronological or logical order.

_____ A few years later, this group became known as U2.

_____ To date, he has received numerous awards with U2, including 22 Grammies (music awards).

_____ Bono was born and raised in Ireland.

_____ In 1976 he became a part of a musical group that began to write their own songs.

_____ In 2007 he was granted an honorary knighthood by Queen Elizabeth for the good work he had done.

_____ His mother died when he was 14; many of the personal songs he has written are about her.

_____ Bono is the main vocalist for the group U2.

_____ He has become well known for organizing and playing in many benefit concerts to help poor and starving people in Africa and South America.

Dictogloss ❀ *Listen to a complete sentence only once and write down the words you can remember on a separate piece of paper. With a partner, try to reconstruct the entire sentence and write it below.*

1.

2.

3.

4.

5.

Discussion ❀ *With a partner, discuss the following questions.*

◆ Have you heard Bono and U2? Do you like the group? Do you have a favorite song?

◆ What groups do you like to listen to?

◆ Do you know of other famous people who devote time to raising money for good causes? Why do you think they do this?

◆ Have you ever been involved in any way in raising money for a good cause?

Follow up ❀ *Choose **one** of these.*

◆ Find out about your favorite group or a group from your country. Present a short description of this group to the class. Play a song by the group.

◆ Use the Internet to find out about other people who have devoted time and energy to fighting poverty, disease, and hunger. Prepare a short presentation of this information to the class.

Ten Interesting Questions

(CD 2 TRACK 16) ♦ *[FULL TEXT 184]*

Introduction ✤

The following ten "dictoglosses" are interesting questions for you and a partner to discuss or even write about.

Dictogloss ✤

Listen to a complete sentence only once and write down the words you can remember on a separate piece of paper. With a partner, try to reconstruct the entire sentence and write it below. After you have done this, discuss each question with your partner.

1.

Question: *Why? Have you ever wished you were the opposite sex?*

2.

Question: *Why?*

3.

Question: *If yes, where would you go? What would you do?*

4.

Question: *If yes, why did you do it?*

5.

Question: *Why?*

6.

Question: *What is one? How do you plan to reach it?*

7.

Question: *Why? Which one affects you the most?*

8.

Question: *Why?*

9.

Question: *Why?*

10:

Question: *Why or why not?*

Discussion ❀ *With a partner, think of some other interesting questions to ask your classmates.*

Follow up ❀ *Choose one or more of the ten interesting questions to write about.*

The Rise of Wives

(CD 2 TRACK 17) ♦ [FULL TEXT 185]

Introduction ❀

Forty years ago, when relatively few wives worked outside the home, their husbands were the main source of income for the family. Marriage enhanced the economic status of women more than that of men. In American society today, however, the economic gains associated with marriage are now greater for men because their college-educated working wives often bring home greater salaries.

Percentage of husbands whose wives have incomes higher than their own	
4%	22%
1970	2007

Dictogloss ❀

Listen to a complete sentence only once and write down the words you can remember on a separate piece of paper. With a partner, try to reconstruct the entire sentence and write it below.

1.

2.

3.

4.

5.

6.

Discussion ❀ *Discuss these questions with a partner. Share your ideas with the class.*

1. Do you see any similar cultural trends in a country you are familiar with? Explain.
2. If a wife made a lot more money than her husband, would that be an issue for:
   a. you?   b. your parents?
3. Under what circumstances could you see a father being a "househusband" either temporarily or permanently?

Follow up ❀ *Write a paragraph explaining your ideas about the question below:*

Do you think there are some fathers who do a better job of parenting than mothers?

Marriage and Divorce

(CD 2 TRACK 18) ♦ *[FULL TEXT 186]*

Introduction ❀

The U.S. Census Bureau recently issued a marriage and divorce report after interviewing 37,000 Americans and studying the data. While most Americans are not surprised to hear that nearly half of first marriages end in divorce, it's interesting to compare those statistics to 1960, when only one in three marriages ended in divorce. Here are some other observations.

Dictation ❀ *Write the correct word or number in the blank space. Correct and discuss the dictation.*

1. People with a college degree _____ _____ _____ _____ and stay married.

2. Among married women ages 25 to _____ with a college degree, 15 _____ _____ _____ divorced within a year, compared with _____ out of 1000 women with just a _____ _____ _____.

3. People's average age at their first marriage _____ to ____ years for women and ____ for men.

4. In the 1950s and 1960s the _____ _____ for women to marry was _____ and for men it was _____.

5. Divorce is least likely to _____ among _____ and most likely to occur among _____ – _____.

Dictogloss ❀

Listen to a complete sentence only once and write down the words you can remember on a separate piece of paper. With a partner, try to reconstruct the entire sentence and write it below.

1.

2.

3.

4.

5.

Discussion ❀ *Discuss these questions with a partner. Share your ideas with the class.*

1. 9 out of 10 Americans are expected to marry in their lifetime. This is a big change from the 1950s, when everyone was expected to get married. What reasons can you give for this change in expectations?

2. Compare the census report above with trends that you see in your country.

3. Marriage is a legal contract. When couples decide to divorce they have to hire a lawyer and go to court to end the contract. Couples must come to an agreement on alimony, property settlement, and child custody and support. Lawyers are needed to settle these problems. What is the procedure in your culture? Do parents ever get joint custody of the children? (divided time between parents) Do fathers ever get custody?

4. Here are some legal grounds for divorce. Which do you think are most common?

Irreconcilable differences	Money	Imprisonment
Drug addiction	Alcoholism	Certain illnesses
Desertion	Adultery	Mental/physical abuse

5. Some Americans who are between the ages of 60 and 80 and who have lost a spouse decide to remarry. Discuss the advantages and disadvantages of remarrying late in life.

6. Describe a typical wedding in your culture.

7. Are arranged marriages common in your culture?

Follow up ❀ *In the following letter, a prediction dictation, fill in the blanks with a word you think is correct. Then check your answers against the recording. When you are done, give advice to this 15-year-old boy.*

Dear Advisor:

My parents ＿＿ divorced. I live ＿＿＿＿ my mother. I spend two weekends ＿＿＿＿＿ month with my dad and one month in ＿＿＿＿ summer with him. I love my ＿＿＿＿＿＿＿, but he has remarried, and I don't really ＿＿＿＿＿ his new wife, Amy. My father is ＿＿＿＿＿ nice to me and takes ＿＿＿＿＿ places, but Amy sort of resents me and I feel ＿＿＿＿＿＿＿＿＿ around her.

   Now that ＿＿ is, I would rather ＿＿＿＿＿＿ more time at home with my friends. I also ＿＿＿＿＿ to get a part-time ＿＿＿＿ this summer. Do you think ＿＿＿＿＿ father will be ＿＿＿＿＿ if I don't visit him this ＿＿＿＿＿＿? What do you think I should do?

                                       Joey in Jamestown

Obesity

(CD 2 TRACK 19) ♦ [FULL TEXT 187]

Introduction ❀

Despite a seeming obsession with their health, diet, and exercise, Americans are getting fatter and fatter. New information shows that almost one-third of all adults in the United States are overweight, and the number of obese people (defined as being 30% over their ideal weight) increased from 12% in 1991 to 25% in 2010.

Dictogloss ❀

Listen to a complete sentence only once and write down the words you can remember on a separate piece of paper. With a partner, try to reconstruct the entire sentence and write it below.

1.

2.

3.

4.

5.

Discussion ❀ *With a partner, discuss these statements.*

1. What diet ads do you see on TV? What time of year do you see more diet ads than usual? Why?

2. Most Americans who go on diet plans and are successful usually gain back the original weight in one to two years. Why do you think this is?

Follow up ❀ *A person on a diet can still go out to a restaurant as long as they are careful. What does this person have to do to stay on the diet? Write a paragraph.*

Television

(CD 2 TRACK 20) ♦ *[FULL TEXT 188]*

Introduction ❀

Since the 1950s, when television became a part of people's lives, there have been debates about whether it has enriched our lives, has caused great harm, or done both.

Work with a partner and read the sentences that outline a brief history of television. Put the sentences in chronological order.

_____ Full-scale commercial TV broadcasting did not begin in the U.S. until right after World War II.

_____ Electronic TV was successfully demonstrated in 1927.

_____ The first TV presidential debate took place between John. F. Kennedy and Richard Nixon.

_____ Color TV was approved in 1964.

_____ High Definition Televisions (HDTVs) allow for convergence between computers, the Internet, and television.

_____ World War II slowed the development of TV as companies turned to producing military equipment.

_____ In 1963, most Americans watched the assassination of John F. Kennedy and his funeral from their living rooms.

_____ Television grew in the 1970s and 1980s with the introduction of many cable channels.

_____ By 1955 half of all U.S. homes had TVs.

_____ For the first time, people were able to watch a war on television – the Vietnam War.

Dictogloss ❀

Listen to a complete sentence only once and write down the words you can remember on a separate piece of paper. With a partner, try to reconstruct the entire sentence and write it below.

1.

2.

3.

4.

5.

6.

Discussion ❀ *With a partner, discuss the following questions.*

♦ How much TV do you watch? Do you think you watch too much TV?
♦ What do you watch? What are your favorite programs?
♦ Do you watch television in English? In your first language? In both?

Follow up ❀ *Choose one.*

♦ Create a poll. With your partner, design five questions to ask five people. Present the information to the class. An example of a question is "How many TVs do you have in your house?"

♦ Choose one of the following topics to write about.

"Television is a waste of time." Do you agree or disagree?

"My favorite program when I was a child was _____."

AIDS

(CD 2 TRACK 21) ◆ *[FULL TEXT 189]*

Introduction ❀

AIDS affects large numbers of people, not only in the United States, but all over the world. In 2007 it was estimated that 33.2 million people lived with the disease worldwide, and that AIDS killed an estimated 2.1 million people, including 330,000 children. AIDS is caused by a virus called human immunodeficiency virus (HIV).

"What do you know about AIDS?" ❀

With a partner or by yourself, answer each of the following four questions by circling one of the letters.

1. A person can become infected with AIDS by
   a. drinking from the same cup as someone with HIV.
   b. hugging and touching someone with HIV.
   c. going swimming with someone with HIV.
   d. none of the above

2. HIV is not present in
   a. sweat
   b. blood
   c. semen and vaginal secretions
   d. breast milk

3. Spread of HIV by sexual transmission can be prevented by
   a. abstinence
   b. practicing mutual monogamy with an uninfected partner.
   c. correct use of latex condoms
   d. all of the above

4. If you were infected with HIV, you might show symptoms
   a. within a few weeks
   b. within a year
   c. in 10 or more years
   d. all of the above

Dictogloss ❀

Listen to a complete sentence only once and write down the words you can remember on a separate piece of paper. With a partner, try to reconstruct the entire sentence and write it below.

1.

2.

3.

4.

5.

Discussion ❀ *Discuss these questions with a partner. Share your ideas with the class.*

♦ Is there a serious AIDS problem in your country? Why or why not?
♦ Where did you learn about AIDS? Were there education programs in any of the schools you went to?
♦ Are there AIDS treatment programs in other countries?
♦ In the United States one of the ways drug addicts get AIDS is by sharing needles. Do you agree that there should be a government program to distribute clean needles to drug addicts?

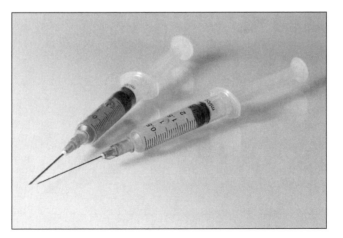

Follow up ❀

*Research **one** of the following and either write a report or report on what you learned to the class.*

1. History of AIDS
2. Medical treatment for AIDS
3. Effects of AIDS on economics and society

Idioms for Test Takers

(CD 2 track 22) ◆ *[Full Text 190]*

Introduction ❀

The English language has thousands of idioms. Here are a few that American students use before or after taking an exam or in a classroom situation. Practice using them with your classmates.

Dictogloss ❀

Listen to a complete sentence only once and write down the words you can remember on a separate piece of paper. With a partner, try to reconstruct the entire sentence and write it below.

1. _____.
   Meaning: I made lots of mistakes; probably failed.

2. _____.
   Meaning: I did poorly; didn't follow directions; made mistakes.

3. _____
   Meaning: I'm sure I did well on the test.

4. _____
   Meaning: I'm very nervous (usually before a test).

5. _____
   Meaning: I'm nervous; tense; jittery.

6. _____
   Meaning: It was an easy test; a cinch.

7. _____
   Meaning: I studied hard for hours last night.

8. _____
   Meaning: It was an easy test.

Discussion ❀ *With the class, respond to these items. Practice saying them.*

1. Which of the idioms above can you use to respond to: "How did you do on the test?" or "What was the test like?"

2. Which of the idioms above can you use to respond to the question "How do you feel?"

Cooperative Learning ❋ Working with idioms

Find the meanings of the following idioms:

Work in four groups of three or four students. Using the Internet, each student finds out about one or more items underlined below and reports back to the group. Then all four groups present what they have learned.

Group 1

1. I got hung up on test question number 4.
2. He's a know-it-all.
3. She's an egghead.
4. We're all on the same wavelength on that issue.

Group 2

1. I was really psyched for the test.
2. After she got her test results, she was jumping for joy.
3. Exhausted after the long test, she went back home and caught some z's.
4. After the easy test, all the students gave each other high fives.

Group 3

1. She's missed so many classes that she doesn't have a prayer of passing the course.
2. He was angry after the test and needed to vent to his friends.
3. When the university discovered he'd cheated on the test, they threw the book at him.
4. She has her hands full trying to finish that research paper in time.

Group 4

1. The teacher gave a pop quiz.
2. I heard through the grapevine that everyone passed the test.
3. He was so tired after the test, he went to bed and was out like a light.
4. She was banking on getting an A in the course.

Follow up ❋

♦ *Make a list of your favorite idioms from this unit and practice pronouncing them.*
♦ *Try to use one at least once a week.*

Make a Difference! Be a Volunteer!

(CD 2 TRACK 23) ♦ *[FULL TEXT 192]*

Introduction ❀

Millions of Americans do volunteer work every day. Some volunteer in schools, libraries, and homeless shelters. Others volunteer during times of disasters such as an earthquake or flood. Here is the story of Perry Flicker, a New Jersey Intel supervisor who offered his services in New York City after 9/11/01.

Work with a partner and read the sentences, which outline a short story of Perry Flicker's volunteer experience. Put them in chronological or logical order.

____ After that first exhausting and terrifying day in ash-covered ruins, he remained there.

____ Perry had done volunteer work before, visiting the sick and lonely senior citizens, but this was a totally new experience for him. This had changed his life forever.

____ "I couldn't get over the humility and compassion for people there," Perry said. "Firefighters and police were risking their lives searching for survivors, and they were thanking me."

_1_ When Perry Flicker saw the World Trade Towers collapse on TV, he couldn't just sit by and watch. He had to do something.

____ When he arrived, there were piles of supplies to be sorted, like flashlights, sweatshirts, gloves, and T-shirts. The supplies just kept coming in.

____ When he heard volunteers were needed to deliver water, Gatorade, power bars, and goggles to the disaster site, he raced from New Jersey to New York.

____ He just kept going. He was up three and a half straight days without sleep.

____ "Thanking ME? That's incredible. Nobody felt like a hero there. We all just felt like people who had something to do."

People like Flicker are ordinary citizens who are considered special because they have done something important for society. They do not receive any payment for their work but give their time, services, and expertise. Every year one American is chosen to receive the U.S.A. Award for making their country a better place to live. You will choose the winner from one of the six finalists below.

Note Taking ❀

Listen and take notes. It is not necessary to write every word, only the information you think is important. When you are finished, go over your notes with a partner to be sure you both have the same information.

1. John Ryan, 48

2. Leon Goldberg, 68

3. LaToya Jefferson, 51

4. Addie May Carlson, 75

5. Bob Dean, 36

6. Lena Chin, 52

Discussion ❀ *Work with a partner and discuss each item. Then share your answers with the class.*

1. Which person did you and your partner choose and why? Share your reasons with the class. Then work with your classmates to decide on one winner.

2. Discuss ways that people in your country help other people without being paid. What kinds of situations encourage volunteers?

3. Americans like to give awards. For example, there are the Academy Awards for actors and actresses, and there are the Grammy awards for musicians, and Best Citizen Awards in some cities and towns. Do people in your home city receive awards for helping other people?

4. After natural disasters like hurricanes and earthquakes, what kinds of organizations help to rescue people?

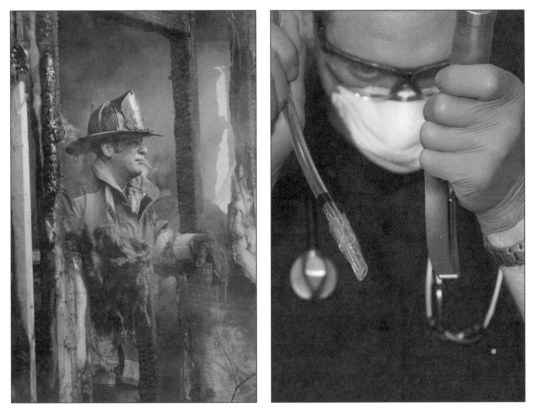

Volunteer Fireman and EMT (Emergency Medical Technician)

Follow up ❀ *Choose **one** of the following:*

1. Write a paragraph explaining why you think the person you chose deserves the U.S.A. award. Begin by describing the situation from your notes.

2. Write about an experience you, a parent, or friend had as a volunteer. What kind of work was it and how long did you do it?

Birthdays Around the World

(CD 2 TRACK 24) ♦ *[FULL TEXT 193]*

Introduction ❀

The tradition of birthday parties started in Europe a long time ago. It was feared that evil spirits were particularly attracted to people on their birthdays. To protect them from harm, friends and family would come to stay with the birthday person and bring good thoughts and wishes. Giving gifts brought even more good cheer to ward off the evil spirits. In this unit, we will discuss different ways birthdays are celebrated throughout the world today.

Note Taking ❀

Listen and take notes. It is not necessary to write every word, only the information you think is important. When you are finished, go over your notes with a partner to be sure you both have the same information.

1. **Germany**

2. **Japan**

3. **Denmark**

4. **England, Canada, Australia, and New Zealand**

5. **China**

6. **Mexico**

Discussion ❀ *With a partner, discuss one of these items.*

If your country is mentioned above, do you agree with what is explained here? If not, explain and give more information about birthdays. Is special food prepared? Are there special gifts or money given? What birthdays are considered "special"?

If your country is not mentioned above, tell your parter about how birthdays in your family are celebrated.

Follow up ❀ *Choose **one** of the following and write a paragraph.*

1. Write about a memorable birthday party OR graduation party.
2. Compare how you celebrate a birthday to one of the countries above.

Cooperative Learning ❀ Birthdays Around the World

Work in four groups of three or four students. Using a world map or the Internet, each student finds out about one or more items listed below and reports back to the group. Then all four groups present what they have learned. Share your answers with the class and point out the locations on the world map.

Group 1

1. Name 4 countries that begin with the letter A.
2. Name 4 cities in the world that begin with the letter A.
3. Name 4 U.S. state capitals that begin with the letter A.
4. Name 4 cities or towns in your state that begin with the letter A.

Group 2

1. Name 4 countries that begin with the letter C.
2. Name 4 cities in the world that begin with the letter C.
3. Name 4 U.S. state capitals that begin with the letter C.
4. Name 4 cities or towns in your state that begin with the letter C.

Group 3

1. Name 4 countries that begin with the letter M.
2. Name 4 cities in the world that begin with the letter M.
3. Name 4 cities in the U.S. that begin with the letter M.
4. Name 4 cities or towns in your state that begin with the letter M.

Group 4

1. Name 4 countries that begin with the letter S.
2. Name 4 cities in the world that begin with the letter S.
3. Name 4 U.S. state capitals that begin with the letter S.
4. Name 4 cities or towns in your state that begin with the letter S.

The People's Court

(CD 2 TRACK 25) ◆ [FULL TEXT 195]

Introduction ❁

People's Courts are also known as Small Claims Courts. These courts are open to anyone who has a disagreement about an amount of money between $500 and $5000. A person does not need a lawyer. A judge listens to the case and makes a common–sense decision. In this chapter you will hear four typical cases that come before these courts.

Note Taking ❁

Listen and take notes. It is not necessary to write every word, only the information you think is important. When you are finished, go over your notes with a partner to be sure you both have the same information.

Case 1

Case 2

Case 3

Case 4

Discussion ❁ *Work with a partner or small group and decide who should pay whom and how much in the four cases above. Try to reach a consensus.*

Follow up ❁ *Write a summary of the four cases and explain your decisions.*

You Be The Judge

(CD 2 track 26) ◆ [Full Text 196]

Introduction ❀

Murder and rape are serious crimes. Robbery and assault are somewhat less serious, but the punishment for all crimes has to follow state law. If a murder has been committed in Texas or Florida, for example, the criminal can receive the death penalty. In Massachusetts, the person would go to prison for life. The punishment for manslaughter (accidental killing) also varies from state to state. The judge decides what is fair. In the note-taking activity there are three punishments some criminals actually received. According to public opinion, these punishments were either too strict or too lenient.

Note Taking ❀

Listen and take notes. It is not necessary to write every word, only the information you think is important. When you are finished, go over your notes with a partner to be sure you both have the same information. When you are finished, discuss each case and decide what punishment you would approve of.

1. **Case One.   New York**

2. **Case Two.   Texas**

3. **Case Three.   Massachusetts**

Discussion ❀ *In a small group, decide on fair punishments for the following crimes. If you think the person should go to prison, decide on how long.*

1. While driving, a mother of five children in Massachusetts accidentally hit a three-year-old child who ran into the street. She was not speeding. The child died two days later.

2. A Florida man was found guilty of kidnapping and killing a nine-year-old girl who was his next-door neighbor. Her mutilated body was found in a field a month later.

Follow up ❀ *Write a summary of the three cases and express your opinion about each one.*

Plastics Alert

(CD 2 TRACK 27) ♦ *[FULL TEXT 197]*

Introduction ❀

We all know that there are certain chemicals in our environment that are harmful to us. One of those toxic carcinogens is called dioxin. Dr. Edward Fujimoto, manager of a wellness program at a hospital, tells us about dioxins and how bad they are for us.

Note Taking ❀

Listen and take notes. It is not necessary to write every word, only the information you think is important. When you are finished, go over your notes with a partner to be sure you both have the same information.

Here are a few words with their abbreviations to help: microwave (mw), release (rls), ceramic (cer), dioxin (dx), heat (ht), cells (cls)

Discussion ❀ *Discuss these questions with a partner. Share your ideas with the class.*

1. If you buy TV dinners, soups, and other foods that come in plastic containers, what two steps should you follow before using your microwave?

2. Americans buy billions of white coffee filters, paper towels, and paper napkins. They are white because they are bleached. The process of bleaching paper is responsible for creating dioxin. What alternatives are there for using these paper products?

3. To make plastic wrap cling, manufacturers add "plasticizers," potentially harmful chemicals that can work their way into your food. This can be even more serious if you use it in a microwave. What alternatives are there for storing leftover food or heating food without this wrap?

4. What other harmful chemicals can you find in your apartment or home? Make a list and compare your answers with the class.

Follow up ❀

In recent years, plastic products have been showing up in the stomachs of whales, and tiny particles have been found in the fish we buy at the supermarket. Do some research on the dangers of plastic in our environment. Write a two-page paper.

Short Business Decisions

(CD 2 TRACK 28) ♦ *[FULL TEXT 198]*

Introduction ❀

Both the owner of a small business and a top executive of a large corporation have to make difficult decisions which will affect the business for better or worse. Decision making is the boss's job.

Note Taking ❀

Listen as your teacher reads three different situations where the boss must make a decision. Take notes. With a partner, check your notes and decide what the boss should do.

Situation 1

Julia

Margaret

Richard

Situation

Decision

Situation 2

Charles

Town official

Situation

Decision

Situation 3

Jack

Louise

Situation

Decision

Discussion ❀ *With a partner, discuss the following questions.*

♦ Do you think that giving bribes to officials is a common practice in many countries?

♦ Have you ever had to make an important decision? Tell your partner about it.

Follow up ❀ *Choose* **one** *of the following.*

1. With your partner, create a business scenario where the boss has to make a decision. Act it out for the class and have them make the decision.

2. Write about a difficult decision you had to make.

Hold the Pickles, Hold the Lettuce

(CD 2 TRACK 29) ◆ *[FULL TEXT 199]*

Introduction ❀

The McDonald's Corporation has become a powerful symbol of America's service economy, the sector now responsible for ninety percent of the country's new jobs. In 1968, McDonald's operated about 1,000 restaurants. By the year 2000 it had about 23,000 restaurants worldwide and was opening roughly 2,000 new ones each year. There are now more than 31,000 McDonald's restaurants worldwide.

Prediction Dictation ❀

*In this dictation you are **not** going to listen first. Work with a partner and fill in each blank with a word you think is correct. When you are finished, you will listen and do the dictation on the next page. Then compare your responses.*

What is perhaps _____ astonishing about America's fast _____ business is just how successful it _____ become: what began in the 1940s as a handful of hot dog and hamburger stands in Southern California _____ spread across the land to become a $110 billion industry. _____ _____ Eric Schlosser, the author of *Fast Food Nation,* _____ now spend more on _____ _____ _____ they spend on higher _____, personal computers, _____ software, or new cars, or on movies, books, videos, and recorded music combined. Mr. Schlosser writes that on any given day in the _____ _____ about one quarter of the adult population visits a fast food _____, and that the typical _____ now consumes approximately three hamburgers and four orders of French _____ every week.

"An estimated one of _____ eight workers in the United States has at some time been employed _____ McDonald's," he adds, and the company hires more _____ than any other American organization, public or _____.

As fast _____ franchises from McDonald's to Pizza _____ to KFC go global, this dynamic has assumed international flavor. In Brazil, Mr. Schlosser reports, McDonald's _____ _____ the nation's largest private employer. _____ at McDonald's Hamburger University in Oak Park, Illinois, are now taught in 20 different _____, and a Chinese anthropologist notes that all the _____ in a primary school in Beijing recognized an image of Ronald McDonald. For the _____, the anthropologist noted, McDonald's represents "Americana and the promise of modernization."

Listening Dictation ❀ *Write the correct word in the blank space. Correct and discuss the dictation.*

What is perhaps _____ astonishing about America's fast _____
business is just how successful it _____ become: what began in the 1940s as
a handful of hot dog and hamburger stands in Southern California _____
spread across the land to become a $110 billion industry. _____ _____ Eric
Schlosser, the author of *Fast Food Nation,* _____ now spend more on
_____ _____ _____ they spend on higher _____,
personal computers, _____ software, or new cars, or on movies, books,
videos, and recorded music combined. Mr. Schlosser writes that on any given day in
the _____ _____ about one quarter of the adult population visits a
fast food _____, and that the typical _____ now consumes
approximately three hamburgers and four orders of French _____ every week.

"An estimated one of _____ eight workers in the United States has at
some time been employed _____ McDonald's," he adds, and the company hires more
_____ than any other American organization, public or _____.

As fast _____ franchises from McDonald's to Pizza _____ to KFC go global,
this dynamic has assumed international flavor. In Brazil, Mr. Schlosser reports,
McDonald's _____ _____ the nation's largest private employer.
_____ at McDonald's Hamburger University in Oak Park, Illinois, are now
taught in 20 different _____, and a Chinese anthropologist notes that all the
_____ in a primary school in Beijing recognized an image of Ronald
McDonald. For the _____, the anthropologist noted, McDonald's
represents "Americana and the promise of modernization."

Discussion ❀ *Discuss these questions with a partner. Share your ideas with the class.*

1. Why do you think fast food restaurants are so popular? Can you list five reasons?

2. What do critics of fast food restaurants say about them? Can you list five criticisms?

3. Are there American fast food restaurants in your country or a country you have visited? Do they have different items on the menu because they are in a different country? Do you have fast food restaurants that are specific to that country?

4. What is your favorite fast food restaurant and what is your favorite meal?

Follow up ❀ *Work with a partner and see if you know the meaning of the following. Do you know any other idiomatic food expressions that you can add to this list?*

1. Hold the pickles, hold the lettuce.
2. I want that "to go."
3. Go easy on the salt.
4. Light on the dressing.
5. I'll have it medium rare.
6. I want my eggs sunny side up.
7. I'll have my eggs over easy.
8. I'll have my coffee black.
9. Heavy on the pickles, please.
10. I'll have a breast and a leg.
11. I'd like my dressing on the side.
12. Give me the works.

Babe Didrikson Zaharias *(1911-1956)*

(CD 2 TRACK 30) ♦ *[FULL TEXT 201]*

Introduction ❀

Mildred Ella "Babe" Didrikson Zaharias was an American athlete who excelled in every sport she tried. She was a track and field champion, an All-American basketball star, a record-setting golfer, and all-around force in everything from baseball to bowling. Here is a short biography of a woman who was named one of the greatest athletes of the 20th century.

Prediction Dictation ❀

In this activity, you are not going to listen first. Work with a partner or alone, and fill in each blank with a word you think is correct. When you are finished, listen and do the dictation on the next page. Then compare your answers.

When Babe Didrikson was ___ teenager in 1925, she knew her life's ambition. "My goal was to be the _____athlete who ever lived," she said.

Her parents _____ hard-working immigrants _____ Norway, and Babe grew up in a tough working-class environment that helped shape her independent _____ self-reliant spirit. A tomboy, she was strong and driven _____ assert herself. In elementary school _____ was dubbed "Babe" after Babe Ruth because of her athletic _____ on the baseball field.

In school, she dominated _____sport she tried: volleyball, tennis, baseball, swimming, and especially basketball, which was very _____ among young women at the time. At _____ 18, she was recruited to _____ a company's professional basketball team, where she quickly _____the star. Soon after, she amazed audiences _____ many track and field events as well. In the 1932 Olympics she won several gold _____ for track and field.

While Babe was a natural athlete, it was_____ incredible determination that made her a champion. Her next _____to tackle was golf, where she _____ an

unstoppable force, winning 82 tournaments _____ the 30s and 40s. She co-founded the
Ladies Professional Golf Association (LPGA), a world-wide_____.

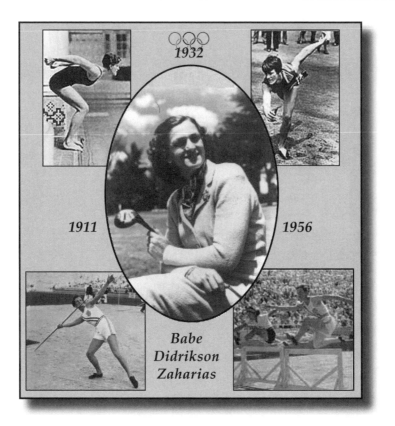

1932

1911   1956

Babe
Didrikson
Zaharias

On the golf course she _____ George Zaharias, a Greek-American, in 1938. They
married and Babe took and _____ her husband's name, but by then the Didrikson
name _____ famous.

Didrikson was at _____ top of her career in the early 50s, and with all her tour
winnings _____ endorsements, she was _____ over $100,000 a year, an
incredible _____ for a woman athlete of that time. But in 1953, she faced a major
_____ she couldn't overcome – colon cancer. After the surgery, _____ said
she'd be too weak to _____ sports, but four months later she was _____ in golf
tournaments. And in 1954 she _____ winning again. She continued playing
until 1955, when _____ the cancer returned. She held on for another year.
Didrikson, arguably _____ _____ _____ greatest athletes of the twentieth century,
_____ on September 27, 1956.

Listening Dictation ❧ *Listen and fill in the blanks with the words you hear. Then, with a partner, compare your prediction to the dictation.*

When Babe Didrikson was ___ teenager in 1925, she knew her life's ambition. "My goal was to be the _____athlete who ever lived," she said.

Her parents _____ hard-working immigrants _____ Norway, and Babe grew up in a tough working-class environment that helped shape her independent _____ self-reliant spirit. A tomboy, she was strong and driven _____ assert herself. In elementary school _____ was dubbed "Babe" after Babe Ruth because of her athletic _____ on the baseball field.

In school, she dominated _____sport she tried: volleyball, tennis, baseball, swimming, and especially basketball, which was very _____ among young women at the time. At _____ 18, she was recruited to _____ a company's professional basketball team, where she quickly _____the star. Soon after, she amazed audiences _____ many track and field events as well. In the 1932 Olympics she won several gold _____ for track and field.

While Babe was a natural athlete, it was_____ incredible determination that made her a champion. Her next _____to tackle was golf, where she _____ an unstoppable force, winning 82 tournaments _____ the 30s and 40s. She co-founded the Ladies Professional Golf Association (LPGA), a world-wide_____.

On the golf course she _____ George Zaharias, a Greek-American, in 1938. They married and Babe took and _____ her husband's name, but by then the Didrikson name _____ famous.

Didrikson was at _____ top of her career in the early 50s, and with all her tour winnings _____ endorsements, she was _____ over $100,000 a year, an incredible _____ for a woman athlete of that time. But in 1953, she faced a major

_____ she couldn't overcome – colon cancer. After the surgery, _____ said she'd be too weak to _____ sports, but four months later she was _____ in golf tournaments. And in 1954 she _____ winning again. She continued playing until 1955, when _____ the cancer returned. She held on for another year. Didrikson, arguably _____ _____ _____ greatest athletes of the twentieth century, _____ on September 27, 1956.

Discussion ❀

Here are some sports Babe played. Can you guess what each sport is?

1. After she knocked down all the pins for a strike, she won the game.

2. All the fans had their eyes on the mound, waiting to see what the nervous pitcher would do.

3. She dribbled as she ran down the court.

4. She did 20 laps in the pool every day.

5. She and her friend picked up their racquets and went to the court.

6. She swung her driver, and the ball sailed in the air and landed on the green.

7. She ran down the track, leaned on her pole, and flew over the bar.

8. She liked to do three miles a day. It usually took her about 20 minutes.

Follow up ❀

*Here are some other outstanding female athletes. Choose **one** and find out more information about her. Report back to the class.*

Jackie Joyner-Kersee	Annika Sorenstam	Michelle Wie
Althea Gibson	Wilma Rudolph	Venus Williams
Michelle Kwan	Lorena Ochoa	Mia Hamm

Cults on Campus

(CD 2 track 31) ◆ [Full Text 202]

Introduction ❃

A cult is an organization. It is frequently religious in nature, and it often follows strange customs and practices. Cults recruit millions of smart people each year. They particularly like to prey on college students and people from other countries, because people in transition are often looking for groups to join. In this dictation, two college students, Shawn and Karen, share their experiences with a cult recruiter.

Prediction Dictation ❃

In this dictation you are not going to listen first. Work alone or with a partner and fill in each blank with a word you think is correct. When you are finished, you will listen and do the dictation on the next page. Then compare your responses.

Shawn, student at UCLA:

In the middle of my freshman year, I _____ having a tough time socially, since I broke up _____ my girlfriend and _____ roommate was always out with friends. So when this friendly-looking _____ came up to me on campus, _____ caught me when I was in a real funk. He was very _____ and polite, and we talked _____ campus issues and friends. After a while he _____ me to think about coming _____ joining a group he was in where I could make some new _____.

I decided to give it a shot. But when I was _____ the second long "meeting" I _____ to feel I was getting sucked into something I wasn't _____ about . . . like they _____ making me feel guilty and ashamed about everything I _____. Then they made some remarks _____ how I'd be better off limiting contact with _____ and friends. Even though I _____ feeling depressed, it didn't feel _____. I felt a tremendous relief when I decided not to go _____.

Karen, student at NYU:

When I arrived here, I was _____ excited about coming to a new city to _____. It was my first time away _____ home and I was psyched to break away from my _____ life and meet new _____. One day _____ the cafeteria, a nice-looking guy, who I _____ was a student, approached me and _____ got talking. At first _____ was about family and friends, _____ we really seemed _____ hit it off, but later on into _____ conversation, I figured out that he _____ _____ a student here. Then he started making suggestions that I _____ to his church club, where I could _____ new friends. After a half hour _____ was getting really bad vibes about the _____ he tried to latch on to me. Finally, I told _____ to get lost. When I _____ about this in my journal to my English professor, she _____ me that there are _____ 3000 cults operating in the U.S., and that the fastest-growing _____, the International Churches of Christ, _____ been banned from at least 39 colleges.

Listening Dictation ❀ *Listen and fill in the blanks with the words you hear. Then with a partner, compare your prediction to the listening.*

Shawn, student at UCLA:

In the middle of my freshman year, I _____ having a tough time socially, since I broke up _____ my girlfriend and _____ roommate was always out with friends. So when this friendly-looking _____ came up to me on campus, _____ caught me when I was in a real funk. He was very _____ and polite, and we talked _____ campus issues and friends. After a while he _____ me to think about coming _____ joining a group he was in where I could make some new _____. I decided to give it a shot. But when I was _____ the second long "meeting" I _____ to feel I was getting sucked into something I wasn't _____ about . . . like they _____making me feel guilty and ashamed about everything I _____. Then they made some remarks _____ how I'd be better off limiting contact with _____ and friends. Even though I _____ feeling depressed, it didn't feel _____. I felt a tremendous relief when I decided not to go _____.

Karen, student at NYU:

When I arrived here, I was _____ excited about coming to a new city to _____. It was my first time away _____ home and I was psyched to break away from my _____ life and meet new _____. One day _____ the cafeteria, a nice-looking guy, who I _____ was a student, approached me and _____ got talking. At first _____ was about family and friends, _____ we really seemed_____ hit it off, but later on into _____ conversation, I figured out that he _____ _____ a student here. Then he started making suggestions that I _____ to his church club, where I could _____ new friends. After a half hour _____ was getting really bad vibes about the _____ he tried to latch on to me. Finally, I told _____ to get lost. When I _____ about this in my journal to my English professor, she _____ me that there are _____ 3000 cults operating in the U.S., and that the fastest-growing _____, the International Churches of Christ, _____ been banned from at least 39 colleges.

Discussion 1 ❀ *With a partner, talk about these issues.*

1. What are the dangers of cults?

2. Why do many cults have "church" names?

Discussion 2 ❀ *Discuss these questions with a partner. Share your ideas with the class.*

1. Do you know of any cults in the U.S. or in your country? What are the purposes of these cults and who are their targets?

2. What techniques do you think cults use to attract people?

3. Why are high-pressure groups so harmful?

4. Some campuses have support groups for victims of cults. What type of person would be vulnerable to joining a cult?

5. How can you tell the difference between a legal religious group and a cult group?

6. Not all cults have religious names or associations. There are other high-pressure groups that can also require total devotion, but instead of a religious agenda, preach revolution, wealth, racism, witchcraft, or superiority. Do you know of any of these groups?

7. What are some reasons why cults continue to survive?

Follow up ❀ *Discuss the following paragraph and questions. Share your ideas with the class.*

A husband and wife who belong to a fundamentalist religious sect based in Attleboro, Massachusetts, were charged with the murder of their 10-month-old son, who police believe died of starvation. The parents were accused of withholding food and secretly burying their baby in a wooded area. Members of this sect do not believe in traditional medicine or the American legal system. The police became involved to protect present and future children of this particular group. The husband and wife are in their mid-thirties.

Do you think the state should step in and prosecute the sect? Why or why not?

Winning in Las Vegas

(CD 2 TRACK 32) ♦ [FULL TEXT 203]

Introduction ❀

Have you ever won money in a lottery or card game, or at a gambling casino? Many people go to Las Vegas with the dream of winning "big bucks." Here is a letter to the advice columnist, Ann Landers, from a woman who really did win, but then her problems began!

Prediction Dictation ❀

In this dictation you are not going to listen first. Work alone or with a partner and fill in each blank with a word you think is correct. When you are finished, you will listen and do the dictation on the next page. Then compare your responses.

I need an unbiased person with a good set of brains to help _____ sort this out. A woman I work _____ (we're compatible friends) decided we should _____ our vacation together and _____ to Las Vegas and gamble, just for the heck of it. Nellie _____ I saved all year and each of us _____ able to _____$1800 for the trip. After travel and hotel expenses, we _____ just $400 left for gambling.

Nellie and I _____ a terrific time, saw some _____ shows, and ate like royalty. We lost some _____ at blackjack and the craps tables so _____ stopped and went for _____ slot machines, which we _____ love. We each had $100 left, _____ decided to _____ the one-dollar machines.

By 2:30 a.m. we _____ exhausted , and all the money we had set aside for _____ was gone. Nellie started to walk _____ to our rooms. I then said, "I'm going to _____ one last dollar in _____ call it quits." I stepped over to the _____ that Nellie had been feeding all night, put in a _____ and lo and behold, I hit the jackpot! The _____ was falling all over the floor, and it _____ like an endless stream of silver dollars was _____ out. I counted the total and it _____ to $1200.

Nellie _____, "You have to split that with me. I fed that machine _____

night!" I replied, "When you _____ away, it became MY machine. I don't owe

you _____." She yelled, "What kind of _____ are you anyway?"

Well, I _____ our friendship was at stake, and _____ to split

my winnings with Nellie. I _____ like to know, was I a fool to _____ it,

or was I morally obligated _____ share my winnings? Please tell me what you

_____.

Tess in Texas

Listening Dictation ❀ *Listen and fill in the blanks with the words you hear. Then with a partner, compare your prediction to the listening.*

I need an unbiased person with a good set of brains to help _____ sort this out. A woman I work _____ (we're compatible friends) decided we should _____ our vacation together and _____ to Las Vegas and gamble, just for the heck of it. Nellie _____ I saved all year and each of us _____ able to _____$1800 for the trip. After travel and hotel expenses, we _____ just $400 left for gambling.

Nellie and I _____ a terrific time, saw some _____ shows, and ate like royalty. We lost some _____ at blackjack and the craps tables so _____ stopped and went for _____ slot machines, which we _____ love. We each had $100 left, _____ decided to _____ the one-dollar machines.

By 2:30 a.m. we _____ exhausted , and all the money we had set aside for _____ was gone. Nellie started to walk _____ to our rooms. I then said, "I'm going to _____ one last dollar in _____ call it quits." I stepped over to the _____ that Nellie had been feeding all night, put in a _____, and lo and behold, I hit the jackpot! The _____ was falling all over the floor, and it _____ like an endless stream of silver dollars was _____ out. I counted the total and it _____ to $1200.

Nellie _____, "You have to split that with me. I fed that machine _____ night!" I replied, "When you _____ away, it became MY machine. I don't owe you _____." She yelled, "What kind of _____ are you anyway?" Well, I _____ our friendship was at stake, and _____ to split my winnings with Nellie. I _____ like to know, was I a fool to _____ it, or was I morally obligated _____ share my winnings? Please tell me what you _____.

Tess in Texas

Discussion ❀ *Discuss these questions with a partner or small group.*

1.   Think of a response to Tess in Texas, and then share it with the class.

2.   Tell what you know about these different forms of gambling.

Casino gambling	Dog races	State lotteries
Horse races	Card games	Sports betting

3.   What about in another country? Is gambling legal? Give reasons why it is not legal in some countries.

Follow up ❀ *Write a response to Tess and explain your reasons.*

The Olympic Games

(CD 2 TRACK 33) ♦ *[FULL TEXT 204]*

Introduction ❀

Every two years, the Winter or the Summer Olympic Games are offered, and they are watched enthusiastically by over three billion people around the world. Athletes from many different countries compete in the games. Can you name some famous Olympians from your country? Here is a brief history of the Ancient and Modern Games.

Prediction Dictation ❀

In this activity, fill in the blanks before listening to the dictation. Then listen to the same article, write the dictation on the next page, and compare your responses.

The Ancient Games   *Olympia, Greece*

Ancient Greece gave birth to the Olympics more than 2000 years _____ in 776 B.C.

The Games ended in 394 A.D. During those 1000 years, the Ancient Games _____

festivals to honor the many gods that Greeks _____. Olympia, the town

where the most powerful god, Zeus, was worshiped, _____ the first Olympics.

The first Olympic Games consisted of no more than _____ foot race, but as the

Games _____ more popular, other events were _____, such as

horse racing, boxing, chariot racing, and wrestling.

Young men of wealth dominated the early Games, but later, as other sports festivals

became more and more popular and offered big cash _____ to winners, men

of all _____ of society could make sports a _____ – _____ career.

The Olympic Games never offered cash prizes; it was the _____ of winning

that meant everything to young men ages 12 to 17.

The Modern Games

The Olympics were _____ in 1896 and were held every four years. The

Modern Games were later _____ into the Winter and _____

Games. Now the Winter and Summer Games alternate every two _____.

Fewer countries and sports are represented at the Winter Games because fewer

_____come from countries with high mountains and snowfields. The

Summer Games _____thousands of athletes from over 200 countries and

include many more types of sports, _____ _____ swimming and running.

Many Olympic athletes today think of the Olympics as more than just _____

the gold, silver, or bronze _____. They _____ that doing your

personal best brings respect and understanding for _____ athletes playing the

same game for peace _____ humanity.

Listening Dictation ❀ *Write the correct word in the blank space. Correct and discuss the dictation.*

The Ancient Games

Ancient Greece gave birth to the Olympics more than 2000 years _____ in 776 B.C. The Games ended in 394 A.D. During those 1000 years, the Ancient Games _____ festivals to honor the many gods that Greeks _____. Olympia, the town where the most powerful god, Zeus, was worshiped, _____ the first Olympics. The first Olympic Games consisted of no more than _____ foot race, but as the Games _____ more popular, other events were _____, such as horse racing, boxing, chariot racing, and wrestling.

Young men of wealth dominated the early Games, but later, as other sports festivals became more and more popular and offered big cash _____ to winners, men of all _____ of society could make sports a _____ – _____ career. The Olympic Games never offered cash prizes; it was the _____ of winning that meant everything to young men ages 12 to 17.

The Modern Games

The Olympics were _____ in 1896 and were held every four years. The Modern Games were later _____ into the Winter and _____ Games. Now the Winter and Summer Games alternate every two _____. Fewer countries and sports are represented at the Winter Games because fewer _____come from countries with high mountains and snowfields. The Summer Games _____thousands of athletes from over 200 countries and include many more types of sports, _____ _____ swimming and running. Many Olympic athletes today think of the Olympics as more than just _____ the gold, silver, or bronze _____. They _____ that doing your personal best brings respect and understanding for _____ athletes playing the same game for peace _____ humanity.

Discussion ❧

1. *Class Contest.* Work with a partner and list as many different events as you can as quickly as you can. One column will be for Winter Sports and the other column will be for Summer Sports. The pair with the most sports wins the contest. You can also choose Olympic sports not included here.

   Here are some sports in no particular order. You may add your own.

Snowboarding	Figure skating	Gymnastics
Curling	Rowing	Beach volleyball
Rollerblading	Ice hockey	Luge
Table tennis	Fencing	Bobsled
Weight lifting	Downhill skiing	Soccer
Speed skating	Wrestling	Field hockey
Martial arts	Horseback riding	Bicycling

2. From the list above, which sports do you think have been added in the past twenty years?

3. Can you name the top ten medal-winning countries in the most recent Winter Olympics? Here are 18 countries. Find the top ten. Guess if you don't know. You get extra credit if you can name the country with the most gold medals.

Russia	Austria	South Korea	Japan	China	The United States
Canada	Sweden	Germany	Italy	Norway	The Netherlands
Jamaica	Serbia	Switzerland	France	Ukraine	Poland

4. The following countries entered teams that qualified for the first time in the Winter Olympics in Vancouver, Canada. They are: Colombia, Peru, Ghana, Serbia, Montenegro, Cayman Islands, and Pakistan. Which countries do not have a cold climate?

5. Check your dictation of the Ancient Olympics. Which sport is no longer represented in the Olympics?

Follow up ❧ *Find out where the 2014, 2016, and 2018 games will be held. Then choose a country for the following:*

Summer 2020 _____

Winter 2022   _____

Summer 2024 _____

Winter 2026   _____

Election Day in the U.S.A.

(CD 2 TRACK 34) ◆ *[FULL TEXT 206]*

Introduction ❊

What do you know about presidential elections in the U.S.? In what month are presidential elections held? How often are presidents elected? How long can presidents serve?

Prediction Dictation ❊ *In this activity, fill in the blanks before listening to the dictation. Then listen to the same article, write the dictation on the next page, and compare your responses.*

In the United States, presidential _____ are held every four years.

They are always _____ on the first Tuesday after the first Monday in the month of

_____. In most states, Election Day is not a holiday from _____ or

school. The president and the vice-president are _____ for four years. Only

natural-born _____ of the United States are _____ to be president.

Presidents are _____ to be at least thirty-five years old.

There are two major political _____, the Democratic Party _____

the Republican Party. The vice-presidential _____ are selected by

the presidential candidates. Both people are nominated by their _____

parties at national conventions several months _____ Election Day.

On Election Day, _____ of Americans go to the polls to

_____. Polls are_____ in schools, churches, and public

buildings. Polls are _____ from early in the morning until 7:00 or 8:00 in the

_____. Most polls use a _____ machine. People always

_____ by secret ballot.

Today, all United States _____ 18 and _____ can

vote if they want to. In presidential elections, _____ 50–60% of Americans

of voting age vote. On election night the votes are tabulated by _____, and

the winner is usually _____ by midnight.

Listening Dictation ❀ *Write the correct word in the blank space. Correct and discuss the dictation.*

In the United States, presidential _____ are held every four years.
They are always _____ on the first Tuesday after the first Monday in the month of
_____. In most states, Election Day is not a holiday from _____ or
school. The president and the vice-president are _____ for four years. Only
natural born _____ of the United States are _____ to be president.
Presidents are _____ to be at least thirty-five years old.

There are two major political _____, the Democratic Party _____
the Republican Party. The vice-presidential _____ are selected by
the presidential candidates. Both people are nominated by their _____
parties at national conventions several months _____ Election Day.

On Election Day, _____ of Americans go to the polls to
_____. Polls are_____ in schools, churches, and public
buildings. Polls are _____ from early in the morning until 7:00 or 8:00 in the
_____. Most polls use a _____ machine. People always
_____ by secret ballot.

Today, all United States _____ 18 and _____ can
vote if they want to. In presidential elections, _____ 50 to 60% of Americans
of voting age vote. On election night the votes are tabulated by _____, and
the winner is usually _____ by midnight.

Discussion 1 ❀ *Interview your teachers and report your findings to the class. Put a check on the line.*
Ask: "Which party, Republican or Democrat, is more likely to. . ."

	Rep.	Dem.
— support abortion rights	____	____
— support gun control	____	____
— support the death penalty	____	____

Discussion 2 ✤

*Here is a list of issues that American voters think about before they vote. In Column A, read the issues and check the five **you** think are the most important. In Column B, do the same for the five issues you think __Americans__ would consider the most important. Compare your answers with others.*

COLUMN A	COLUMN B
____ protect the environment	___ protect the environment
____ support abortion	___ support abortion
____ improve education for all	___ improve education for all
____ offer a fair tax system	___ offer a fair tax system
____ balance the federal budget	___ balance the federal budget
____ fight terrorism	___ fight terrorism
____ ensure prosperity	___ ensure prosperity
____ ensure a strong military defense	___ ensure a strong military defense
____ improve the health care system	___ improve the health care system

Discussion 3 ✤

On Election Day, Americans do not vote only for political leaders. They also vote on issues such as taxes and gun control. Here are some political and economic issues that Americans discuss and make decisions on. Look at these issues with your partner and decide if you agree or disagree and give reasons why. What issues do you think are most important?

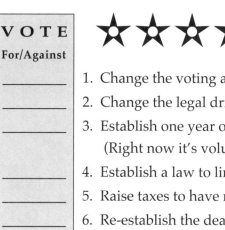

V O T E
For/Against

_____

_____

_____

_____

_____

_____

1. Change the voting age from 18 to 21 years of age.

2. Change the legal drinking age from 21 to 18.

3. Establish one year of mandatory military service for every 18-year-old.
   (Right now it's voluntary.)

4. Establish a law to limit the number of immigrants who can enter the U.S.

5. Raise taxes to have more money for the military and space programs.

6. Re-establish the death penalty in all 50 states.

Follow up ✤ *Write a paragraph in response to one of these questions.*

1. Are there any/many women political leaders in your country or another country you know about? Why/why not?

2. What are some different ways leaders are chosen in the world?

3. Are you interested in politics? Why or why not?

Learning Styles

(CD 2 track 35) ♦ *[Full Text 207]*

Introduction ❀

According to psychologists we learn in many different ways, and learning styles are simply different approaches or ways of learning. Some people are visual learners and learn best through seeing. Some people are auditory learners who learn best through listening. And others are tactile/kinesthetic learners who learn best through moving, doing, and touching. In order to reach all learners, teachers should consider the different learning styles of students when they plan lessons.

Prediction Dictation ❀

In this dictation you are not going to listen first. Work by yourself or with a partner and fill in each blank with a word you think is correct. When you are finished, listen and do the dictation on the next page. Then compare your answers.

Here is a description of one kind of _____, the logical learner. These people _____ very mathematically inclined. _____ enjoy problems, particularly if they are math-related. They are similar to Mr. Spock on _____ _____ because they are very logical, straightforward types _____ learners. They always want to know _____ things work, how things relate to one _____, and why things are here. When they were _____, their favorite toys were building blocks and puzzles. Many of them are now engineers.

Psychologists will give _____ a learning style inventory test to see what _____ of a learner you _____. Here are a _____ examples of statements that could be on these _____.

♦ I prefer to fiddle with things while I listen to or talk _____ people.

♦ I prefer to _____ a map rather than listen to _____ giving me directions.

♦ I enjoy doing more than one thing _____ _____ time.

Listening Dictation ❀ *Listen and fill in the blanks with the words you hear. Then compare your prediction to the listening dictation.*

Here is a description of one kind of _____, the logical learner. These people

_____ very mathematically inclined. _____ enjoy problems, particularly if

they are math-related. They are similar to Mr. Spock on _____ _____ because

they are very logical, straightforward types _____ learners. They always want to know

_____ things work, how things relate to one _____, and why things are here.

When they were _____, their favorite toys were building blocks and puzzles.

Many of them are now engineers.

Psychologists will give _____ a learning style inventory test to see what _____

of a learner you _____. Here are a _____ examples of statements that could be

on these _____.

◆ I prefer to fiddle with things while I listen to or talk _____ people.

◆ I prefer to _____ a map rather than listen to _____ giving me directions.

◆ I enjoy doing more than one thing _____ _____ time.

Learning Style Inventory Test:

Do the following short learning style inventory test to determine if you are an Auditory Learner or a Visual Learner. Write A or V in the space.

1. I would prefer to _____

   follow a set of oral directions *(auditory)*
   follow a set of written directions *(visual)*

2. I would prefer to _____

   attend a lecture given by a famous psychologist *(auditory)*
   read an article written by a famous psychologist *(visual)*

3. I am better at _____

   remembering names *(auditory)*
   remembering faces *(visual)*

4. It is easier to learn new information _____

   using language *(auditory)*
   using images *(visual)*

5. I prefer classes in which the instructor _____

   lectures and answers questions *(auditory)*
   uses films and videos *(visual)*

6. To obtain information about current events
   I would prefer to _____

   watch TV news *(auditory)*
   read the newspaper *(visual)*

7. To learn how to use a new machine I would prefer to _____
   go to a demonstration *(auditory)*
   consult a manual *(visual)*

Score **Auditory** _____ **Visual** _____

A score of 4 to 3 might indicate being one kind of learner or another; obviously greater differences in a score show such a tendency more clearly.

Discussion ❀ *Discuss these questions with a partner. Share your ideas with the class.*

♦ Do you think that the schools you went to affected your learning style?

♦ How can your learning style relate to your study of English?

♦ If you have gone to different schools, were there differences in classroom teaching that affected your learning styles?

♦ Are there any advantages in knowing what your learning style is?

Follow up ❀ *Choose* **one** *of the following.*

1. Go to the Internet. Find other learning style inventory tests. For example, you may find one to determine whether you are a social learner or an independent learner. Take the test yourself. Give the test to a classmate. Tell the class about the test and your results.

2. Research "Multiple Intelligences." Give a short presentation to the class about what you have learned.

3. Write about one of the following topics.

♦ Are you an auditory learner or a visual learner? Give specific examples possibly going back to your childhood.

♦ If you have been to different schools were there differences in classroom teaching? Discuss the differences and how they affected you. Give specific examples.

Bad Hair Day

(CD 2 TRACK 36) ♦ *[FULL TEXT 208]*

Introduction ✿

How our hair looks often affects our perception of ourselves. We often grow our hair, cut our hair, shave our hair, curl our hair, straighten our hair, or change our hair color to look better. Here is a case about hair that actually went to court.

Prediction Dictation ✿

In this dictation you are not going to listen first. Work alone or with a partner and fill in each blank with a word you think is correct. When you are finished, listen and do the dictation on the next page. Then compare your answers.

Albert _____ grown his hair ten inches because he wanted a special hairstyle. He

_____ to a hair _____ that a _____ had recommended and brought

with _____ a photograph _____ a magazine of the style he wanted.

After the _____, he was furious because the _____

had _____ the hair on top of his _____ much _____ short.

His friends made _____ of _____. He had to _____ a

baseball _____ for two _____, day and _____. He was

so _____ that he went to _____ a psychiatrist. Finally he sued

the _____ for ten thousand _____.

You are the judge. What is your _____? Would you make the

_____ pay Albert _____ _____ _____?

Listening Dictation ❀ *Listen and fill in the blanks with the words you hear. Then with a partner, compare your prediction to the listening dictation.*

Albert _____ grown his hair ten inches because he wanted a special hairstyle. He

_____ to a hair _____ that a _____ had recommended and brought

with _____ a photograph _____ a magazine of the style he wanted.

After the _____, he was furious because the _____

had _____ the hair on top of his _____ much _____ short.

His friends made _____ of _____. He had to _____ a

baseball _____ for two _____, day and _____. He was

so _____ that he went to _____ a psychiatrist. Finally he sued

the _____ for ten thousand _____.

You are the judge. What is your _____? Would you make the

_____ pay Albert _____ _____ _____?

Discussion ❀ *With a partner, discuss the following question.*

Should the hairdresser pay Albert? How much? Why?

Follow up ❀ *With a partner, discuss the following ten idioms. What do the expressions mean?*

- ◆ She's having a bad hair day.
- ◆ That movie made my hair stand on end.
- ◆ You need to relax and let your hair down.
- ◆ He won by a hair's breadth.
- ◆ He lost his shirt in the stock market.
- ◆ You'd better sock your money away for a rainy day.
- ◆ Keep this under your hat.
- ◆ He's waiting for the other shoe to drop.
- ◆ She'll go out at the drop of a hat.
- ◆ He's going to throw his hat into the ring.

Exercise

(CD 2 TRACK 37) ♦ *[FULL TEXT 209]*

Introduction ❀

Do you exercise regularly? Do you think about exercising regularly? Do you make resolutions about exercising regularly? The following dictation is from an obituary (a death notice) and it is about an unusual jogger. This dictation may give you a good reason to exercise.

Prediction Dictation ❀ *In this dictation you are not going to listen first. Work alone or with a partner and fill in each word with a word you think is correct. When you are finished, listen and do the dictation on the next page. Then compare your answers.*

Ruth Rothfarb _____ Cambridge was an elderly athlete who inspired many by competing _____ the Boston Marathon (26 miles), the Tufts 10K (10 kilometers), and other long distance _____. Mrs. Rothfarb, who died Wednesday at _____ 96, began running at the age of 69. She began running competitively a few _____ later.

She competed _____ several Boston Marathons and Tufts 10K races as well as long-distance _____ in Atlanta, Los Angeles, New Zealand, and Thailand before her retirement _____ the age of 92. She _____ born in Russia and immigrated _____ the United _____ as a teenager in 1913. After her marriage, she worked full time maintaining a home, raising two _____, and helping her _____ run the family clothing business.

At the age of 67 she found herself with time on her hands after her husband died, their business was sold, and her children were _____. "I had to do something," she _____. "I wasn't going to sit around doing _____."

She began taking walks along the Charles River and around Fresh Pond. When the jogging craze came to her neighborhood, she picked up her speed. "If they can do it, I can _____," she _____. "It's simple enough. All you have to do is pick up your feet and _____."

In 1976 she accompanied her son, Herbert, to a 10K _____. "While everyone was warming up, I asked my _____ if they'd laugh at me if I _____," she said. "He said _____. So I _____. And I finished. It took me a long time, but I _____." She was 75 at the time.

At the age of 84 she was running about 10 miles a _____ and running marathons in about 5 ½ hours. "I like to get going," she said. "If I feel like doing something, I want to do it. I don't have to wait around for anybody else. I don't believe in spending afternoons just _____ around having tea. I do things."

Listening Dictation ❀ *Listen and fill in the blanks with the words you hear. Then with a partner, compare your prediction to the listening dictation.*

Ruth Rothfarb _____ Cambridge was an elderly athlete who inspired many by competing _____ the Boston Marathon (26 miles), the Tufts 10K (10 kilometers), and other long-distance _____. Mrs. Rothfarb, who died Wednesday at _____ 96, began running at the age of 69. She began running competitively a few _____ later.

She competed _____ several Boston Marathons and Tufts 10K races as well as long-distance _____ in Atlanta, Los Angeles, New Zealand, and Thailand before her retirement _____ the age of 92. She _____ born in Russia and immigrated _____ the United _____ as a teenager in 1913. After her marriage, she worked full time maintaining a home, raising two _____, and helping her _____ run the family clothing business.

At the age of 67 she found herself with time on her hands after her husband died,

their business was sold, and her children were _____. "I had to do something," she _____. "I wasn't going to sit around doing _____."

She began taking walks along the Charles River and around Fresh Pond. When the jogging craze came to her neighborhood, she picked up her speed. "If they can do it, I can _____," she _____. "It's simple enough. All you have to do is pick up your feet and _____."

In 1976 she accompanied her son, Herbert, to a 10K _____. "While everyone was warming up, I asked my _____ if they'd laugh at me if I _____," she said. "He said _____. So I _____. And I finished. It took me

a long time, but I _____." She was 75 at the time.

At the age of 84 she was running about 10 miles a _____ and running marathons in about 5 ½ hours. "I like to get going," she said. "If I feel like doing something, I want to do it. I don't have to wait around for anybody else. I don't believe in spending afternoons just _____ around having tea. I do things."

Discussion ❀ *Discuss these questions with a partner. Share your ideas with the class.*

1. Do you exercise? What kind of exercise do you do?

2. Is jogging popular in your country? Who jogs? (age, social class, gender) Where do people jog? What do they wear?

3. When very old people are asked what they think contributed to their long life span, they might answer that a daily glass of red wine was the reason for their reaching 100. What do you think Ruth Rothfarb would answer?

4. Can you think of any negative effects of exercise?

5. Some people love to exercise. Some people hate to exercise. With a partner, read the following quotations, discuss what the writer is saying, and decide whether the writer loves exercise or hates it. Put "L" for "love" and "H" for "Hate."

   _____ a. Those who think they have not time for bodily exercise will sooner or later have to find time for illness. *Edward Stanley*

   _____ b. If it weren't for the fact that the TV set and the refrigerator are so far apart, some of us wouldn't get any exercise at all. *Joey Adams*

   _____ c. My idea of exercise is a good brisk sit. *Phyllis Diller*

   _____ d. I consider exercise vulgar. It makes people smell. *Alex Yuill Thornton*

   _____ e. Lack of activity destroys the good condition of every human being, while movement and methodical physical exercise save it and preserve it. *Plato*

   _____ f. Whenever I feel like exercise, I lie down until the feeling passes. *Robert M. Hutchins*

   _____ g. If your dog is fat, you're not getting enough exercise. *Unknown*

Follow up ❀ *Choose **one** of the following.*

1. With a partner, write some questions about exercise and then poll a group of people. Present your results to the class.

2. Interview someone who has run a marathon and then either write about the interview or present what you have learned to the class.

3. Write about your personal exercise history.

4. Many athletes over the age of 65 compete in marathons. Go to the web and learn about them. Present your information to the class.

5. Obituaries are often little interesting biographies of people who have just died. Find an interesting obituary (in a newspaper) and tell the class about it.

Full Dictation Texts
Immigration Statistics

Partial Dictation ❀ page 1 *(CD 1, track 1)*

1. **During the 1990s** an average of more than **one million immigrants**, legal and **illegal**, settled in the U.S. each year.

2. Legal immigration **fluctuates** between **700,000** and **900,000** each year, and the USCIS estimates that **700,000 illegal immigrants** settle here each year. Most illegal immigrants are from Mexico.

3. In 2008, a record **1,046,539** legal immigrants were naturalized as U.S. **citizens**.

4. **The largest number** of legal immigrants to come between 2001 and 2009 came from **Mexico**, **China**, the Philippines, and **India**.

5. The Census Bureau projects that **by 2050**, one quarter **of the population** will be of **Hispanic descent**.

6. In California, home to over **four million** Asian-Americans, **75%** of all Californians are working for **Asian-owned** businesses or paying rent to an **Asian landlord**.

Open Adoption

Partial Dictation ❋ page 3 *(CD 1, track 2)*

Q. Why did you choose an open adoption?

A. This is a big question, but it **boils down to this**; once we got over the fear that everyone seems to have at first, we **recognized the benefits** of openness. Without the secrecy involved in traditional, **closed type** adoption, there will never be the questions of: "Why did my birthmom **place me here**?" Or, "I wonder **whatever happened** to my baby?" Or, "**Is my baby happy**?" Or, "What kind of woman **gave birth** to this child?" When there are answers **instead of mysteries**, it's better and healthier for everyone.

Q. Aren't you worried that the birthmom will want her baby back?

A. **One of the benefits** of the agency we went with, is the excellent counseling that was provided to both us and our children's birthmoms. **As a result** of this counseling, we were all comfortable with our **situations and decisions**. Because of this comfort, **there was less fear** of a reclaim situation. Also, we knew that the agency we used followed the **legal process** and provided for a fairly secure relinquishment of **birthparents' parental rights**. This was the only way we **would have considered** doing our second adoption.

Q. Are you going to maintain contact with your sons' birthmoms?

A. Yes, we have a very **special relationship** with our sons' birthmoms. We live **fairly close** to Will's birthmom and visit **frequently**. We have been to Will's **half-sister's** birthday party, and they came to Will's first birthday party. We **often exchange** email and cards. Our sons will always have their **birthmoms** in **their lives**, as well as another set of **grandparents**! (There's **no such thing** as too many Grandmas and Grandpas!) Many people seem to think that **having birthparents** involved would **be like co-parenting** or maybe a step-parent relationship. This **is not the case**. We are the "**real** and **forever**" parents of our children.

Note to teachers:

In an open adoption, the amount of time that children are in contact with their birthparents varies quite a bit. In some cases, the birthmother is in contact only once a year because she lives out of state or has married and moved on to start her own family.

In an open adoption, adoptive parents can make initial rejections. For example, if the adoptive baby has parents on drugs, or parents with a history of mental illness or physical or mental abuse, they can tell the agency without any repercussions that they are not interested in that particular baby.

Open adoption agencies can charge between $10,000 and $20,000 for their services. Some of the money goes to the medical fees of the birthmother.

Older children and children with special needs such as mental retardation or those in the Deering family are usually available "free of charge." The state determines when they are legally free for adoption. These children are not part of the open adoption system but are part of a state agency that oversees their welfare.

You may also want to mention that more and more Americans are going abroad to adopt. Discuss the reasons why there are fewer and fewer American children to adopt (because of birth control/abortion and the fact that many girls opt to keep their babies now that it is no longer a scandal).

For more information, students can visit the following web sites:

OpenAdopt.com

Host33.com/scfl/

or e-mail: **scfl@host33.com**

Sexual Orientation: Questions and Answers

Partial Dictation ✿ page 6 *(CD 1, track 3)*

1. What is sexual orientation?

    Sexual orientation is an emotional, **romantic**, or sexual attraction to another person. It includes heterosexuality, homosexuality, and various forms of **bisexuality**. Most scientists today agree that **sexual orientation** is most likely the result of a complex interaction of **biological**, cognitive, and environmental factors. In most people, sexual orientation is shaped **at an early age**.

2. Is sexual orientation a choice?

    No. Human beings cannot choose to be either **gay** or **straight**. Mental health professionals do not consider sexual orientation to be a **conscious choice**. There is considerable evidence to suggest that biology, including **genetic** or **inborn** hormonal factors, plays a significant role in a person's sexuality.

3. Can therapy change sexual orientation?

    No. Even though most homosexuals live **successful, happy** lives, some homosexual or bisexual people may seek to change their sexual orientation through therapy because they are often **pressured** by family members or religious groups to try and to do so. **The reality is** that homosexuality is not an illness. It does not require treatment and **is not changeable**.

4. Is homosexuality a mental disorder or emotional problem?

    No. Psychologists and other **mental health** professionals agree that it is not an illness, mental **disorder**, or emotional problem. **This belief** is based on 35 years of objective, well-designed research.

5. Why is it important for society to be better educated about homosexuality?

    Educating all people about sexual orientation and homosexuality is likely to diminish **anti-gay prejudice**. Accurate information is especially important to young people who are first discovering and **seeking** to **understand** their sexuality – whether homosexual, bisexual, or heterosexual.

6. Is there any legislation against anti-gay violence?

    Yes. Some states include violence **against an individual** on the basis of his or her sexual orientation as a "**hate crime**," and ten U.S. states have laws against discrimination **on the basis of** sexual orientation.

The Psychology of Shopping

Partial Dictation ❀ page 9 *(CD 1, track 4)*

1. Market research **has found** that the **color light purple** makes customers feel like spending money.   *True*

2. Upon entering a store, most customers head **straight ahead**. *False* (They go to the right.)

3. The only reason **that people shop** is that they need something. *False* (They shop when they're depressed, bored, *etc.*)

4. Women have **a greater affinity** for shopping than men.   *True*

5. Express lines **were introduced** to reduce **shopper frustration**.   *True*

6. Online shopping is for the middle and upper classes because you must have a **computer, a bank account**, and a **credit card.**   *True*

7. **Shoes** are **one of the things** bought most online.   *False* (Books are bought most often.)

8. Men purchase or influence purchases **of more than 80%** of all purchases and services. *False* (Women influence 80% of purchases.)

9. Studies show that most people are much less likely to buy, **or less willing to spend** as much when paying with cash **as opposed to** a credit card.   *True*

10. When two women shop together, they often spend less time and money than **when they shop alone**. *False* (They spend more time and more money.)

English Pronunciation and Spelling

Partial Dictation ❀ page 11 *(CD 1, track 5)*

They are too **close** to the door to **close** it.

There was a **row** among the oarsman about how to **row**.

I shed a **tear** about the **tear** in my new shirt.

A farmer can **produce produce**.

The production of produce

The dump was so full, it had to **refuse refuse**.

The **present** is a good time to **present** the **present**.

The insurance for the **invalid** was **invalid**.

The bandage was **wound** around the **wound**.

The soldier decided to **desert** in the **desert**.

Phishing

Partial Dictation ❀ page 12 *(CD 1, track 6)*

1. **Don't reply** to email or pop-up messages that ask for personal or financial information, and **don't click on links** in the message. Don't **cut and paste** a link from the message into your Web browser because phishers **can make links that look as if they go to one site** but actually send you to a different site.

2. Some scammers send an email that **appears to be** from a legitimate business and ask you to call a phone number to **update your account** or access a "**refund**." Don't call this number. If you need to reach an organization **you do business with**, call the number on your financial statements or **on the back of your credit card**.

3. Use **anti-virus** software and anti-spyware as well as a firewall, and update them regularly.

4. Review credit card and **bank account statements** as soon as you receive them to check for **unauthorized charges**.

5. Be careful about opening **any attachment** or downloading any files from emails you receive, regardless of who sent them.

6. **Report phishing emails** to: spam@uce.gov or reportphishing@antiphishing.org.

Discussion answers:

1. Valued Customer; Trusted Bank, Inc.; verify personal information (never give personal information)

2. Spelling mistakes: received, personal, discrepancy.
   Grammar: If this information **is** not correct: may have access**ed** or may have access **to**.

3. Sound legitimate: valued customer; trusted bank; our fraud department.

4. Website is an imaginary one here but if you click on a "real" one and respond, you're phished.

5. You can go to the website Snopes.com, and they will help you.

Source: *Phishing – OnGuard Online* and *Wikipedia*, the free encyclopedia.

Tax Quiz

Partial Dictation ❦ page 14 *(CD 1, track 7)*

1. What percent **of total income** does an average American working couple pay in taxes **every year**?

    a. 38%   b. 25%   c. 12%   d. 59%

    Answer: 38%. A couple earning $25,000 to $30,000 pays more than one-third of its income in taxes. Not all of the 38% is paid as income tax, however. About 15% is income tax, but Americans have to pay a sales tax, excise tax, property tax, and social security, meals, and customs taxes as well!

2. The United States is the country with **the highest taxes**. True or False?

    Answer: False. The U.S. is, in fact, in the middle. Swedish taxpayers pay 53%, Belgians pay 52%, and Germans pay 45%.

3. Where you live **can affect** the amount of tax you pay. True or False?

    Answer: True. Not all states have a sales tax, and those that do have different percentages (from 2% to 8%). Not all states have a state income tax, and those that do have different percentages (Massachusetts 6%, California 11%, New York 15%, and Delaware 16%). Some states with no state income tax are Florida, Nevada, Texas, and Alaska.

4. **Which individual** pays the most in income tax?

    a. single and young   b. married and middle-aged   c. old

    Answer: a. single and young. These people often have lifestyles that expose them to the full force of taxes. Usually they rent instead of owning a house, so they can't take deductions for property taxes and interest on mortgage payments.

5. **From which group of people** do most of the U.S. income taxes come?

   a. People with a salary below $25,000 a year

   b. People with a salary between $25,000 and 50,000

   c. People with a salary above $50,000

   Answer: b. Middle-income people – with a salary between $25,000 and $50,000 – pay more than half of all federal income taxes. The income tax on the low-income group is only about 14% of the federal total, and the upper-income group, though richer, pays only about 25% of the federal total.

6. People making the same income **pay the same income tax.** True or False?

   Answer: False: Deductions for medical bills, dependents, *etc.* make the difference. A man who has a wife and children and has a mortgage on his house and earns $35,000 pays less in taxes than a man who is not married, rents an apartment, and makes the same salary.

7. **The largest percentage** of American tax dollars goes to

   a. national defense   b. health and Medicare   c. transportation

   Answer: b. health and Medicare. Next is the military (national defense).

8. Denmark is a country with very high income taxes, but it also enjoys **low unemployment** and **steady economic growth**. True or False?

   Answer: True: Denmark has recently been named as the country with the happiest citizens.

Trivia Contest

Note to teachers:

1. You can change this dictation to accommodate the interests of your class. For example, the first question is: How many people are there in _____ _____? This answer key will give "the world" but you may want to change it to: New York or Los Angeles. It can be a review of noun clause usage.

2. You can make up your own list of trivia questions. Use information you have covered in previous classes or from recent newspaper reports that they might remember.

Partial Dictation ❊ page 16 *(CD 1, track 8)*

> *Answer key*

1. How many people are there in **the world**? *Six billion*

2. Where are most American cars **manufactured** in the United States? *Detroit*

3. **How often** are presidential **elections held** in the U.S.? *every four years*

4. Who wrote The **Adventures** of Huckleberry **Finn**? *Mark Twain*

5. What does **BLT** mean? *bacon, lettuce, and tomato sandwich*

6. Where can you buy a **Whopper Junior**? *at Burger King*

7. Who is the **richest woman** in the world? *Queen Elizabeth II*

8. In what year did Americans **first land** on the moon? *1969*

9. What is the **most common** first name in the world? *Mohammed*

10. What is the **best-selling** ice cream **flavor** in the U.S.? *Vanilla*

11. How long has your teacher **taught** in this program?

Answers for Cooperative Learning – Trivia Contest

Group 1: 1. Chinese; some Irish; 2. Asks trivia questions; 3. Spanish; 4. Ceylon

Group 2: 1. China, India, Japan; 2. Ecuador; 3. A yellow cake with a creamy filling/ at any U.S. grocery store; 4. John Adams and John Quincy Adams

Group 3: 1. Yuri Gagarin from Russia; 2. Florida and California; 3. 2012 – London, England, and 2016 – Rio de Janeiro, Brazil; 4. French and Arabic

Group 4: 1. 2014 – Sochi, Russia; 2. TV talk show host/actress/entrepreneur; 3. Michael Jackson; 4. She likes candy

A Business That's Going to the Dogs

Partial Dictation ❀ page 18 *(CD 1, track 9)*

Reporter: Richard, how did you get into the **dog day care** business?

Richard: It all started when I agreed to **take care of** a neighbor's dog when she went on vacation for a week. She didn't want to put her dog **in a kennel** and since I have two dogs **of my own**, I said sure. Then when a friend had to take a **business trip** to Texas, he asked me to pet-sit his dogs. Then **word got around**, and more and more working people who worried about their dogs getting lonely during the day started calling me up. **One thing led to another**, and here I am!

Reporter: So how many dogs do you have in your dog day care business now?

Richard: **It varies**; some days we have ten dogs, but we're licensed for **twelve**.

Reporter: Do all of the dogs come for day care while their owners are **at work**?

Richard: No, some come for **overnights or for a week or two** while the owners are on vacation. We have **comfy beds** and **doggie couches**.

Reporter: **That's cool**! What **kind of fees** do you charge?

Richard: If the owner **drops off** his dog, we charge $28.00 a day. If they want **round-trip pick up** in our van, the charge is higher, about 35 **bucks**.

Reporter: You provide transportation?

Richard: Yup. **Drivers** pick up the dogs beginning at 7:30 a.m. from their homes and drop them off at 5:00 p.m. Dogs love **the ride**!

Reporter: Do you have any special **entrance requirements**?

Richard: Well, they have to be **housebroken**, of course. And they must have written proof of rabies and **other inoculations**. Once in a while there's a dog that doesn't **get along with** other dogs, but most love being here with their **buddies**.

Reporter: I can see that you love your job.

Richard: You've **gotta love dogs** to do this. And now that business **is booming**, I can hire more help!

Discussion 1

79% give their pets Christmas or birthday presents

43% cook special food for their cats

33% talk to their pets on the phone or answering machine

84% call themselves the animal's mother or father

21% sometimes dress up their pets for special occasions, such as Halloween

62% sign letters or cards from themselves and their pets

4% send their dogs to dog day care

Answers for Follow up: Animal Idioms

1. To work like a dog = To work hard
2. To put on the dog = To pretend to be important or rich
3. To let sleeping dogs lie = To leave a bad situation alone and not make it worse.
4. To lead a dog's life = To have a miserable life
5. A doggie bag = A bag for uneaten restaurant food to take home "for the dog" – really for the customer.
6. The dog days of summer = Hot, humid, uncomfortable summer weather
7. To let the cat out of the bag = To let a secret be found out
8. Snail mail = regular, not electronic mail

The Trials of Tipping

Partial Dictation ❀ page 22 *(CD 1, track 10)*

"Tipping says **Thank you** for good service," explains Judy Bowman, president of Protocol Consultants International, who **specializes in** training businesses and corporations in business and **dining etiquette**. According to Bowman, the **standard going rate** for tipping has gone up in the last year, from **15** percent to **20** percent. "If you leave a 10 or 15% tip, you're going to get **raised eyebrows**."

The most important thing to remember about tipping is that you tip members of the **service industry** – people who rely on tips to make a living, **not the management**. Think about your waiter as the guy who sits next to you in economics class and your **tipping outlook** may change. Major tipping situations that people **run into** on a regular basis include trips to the **hair salon**, restaurants, taxis, **bars**, and food delivery services. For each service, a basic tip is required, but it's **up to you** to decide how much to give. For someone who goes **above** and **beyond** the call of duty, you would give a tip closer to the 20% range. For example, when ordering a pizza, use the time as a **gauge for tipping**. If you're told the pizza will arrive in 20 minutes, but it comes in 15, you **should tip higher**. On the other hand, if the pizza is late or you've had a **tough time** dealing with the people in the **home** office, you are **completely entitled** to tip **lower** or not at all. If you are not going to tip, **explain why**. This way the delivery guy will know what he's done wrong. The same **rule of thumb** should follow with taxi drivers, hairstylists, and waiters. But if you often go to the same hairstylist or restaurant and the service is good, tip well. The **staff will remember you**!

Answers for Follow up

The following people rarely receive tips:

A security guard, a gas station attendant, a housepainter, a mechanic, a flower delivery person, a mail delivery person, and a package delivery person. However, people delivering hot food like pizza or hotel room service **do** get tipped.

People do not tip their regular mail carrier and package courier or the doorman at their apartment building, but will often give them a gift (usually money) at Christmas.

Do You Believe in Ghosts?

Partial Dictation ❀ page 24 *(CD 1, track 11)*

If you'd like to visit some places in the United States that have a reputation **for being haunted**, you can buy the book, The *National Directory* of *Haunted Places*, by Dennis Hauck, a well-known **authority** on paranormal phenomena. The book contains several thousand **carefully researched** places in countries around the world and mentions many **spooky houses** in the United States.

The most **famous ghost** in the White House in Washington, D.C., one that **has been seen** by presidents and their families on many occasions, is **Abraham Lincoln**, the 16th president, who **was assassinated** in 1865. Lincoln had many tragedies **in his personal life**, one of which was the death of his son, Willie, at age 11. Lincoln believed **in the afterlife** and tried several times to **contact** his son through seances in the White House. Lincoln also had **premonitions** of his own death and once told his secretary that **he knew he** was going to die in office and that he could **envision** his casket in the Rotunda Room of the White House.

Do you think this house is haunted?

Note to teachers: After this unit you may want to play the song or video *Ghostbusters*.

Love Votes

Partial Dictation ❀ page 26 *(CD 1, track 12)*

1. You've **accepted a date** when someone you **really** like calls you **up** and **asks** you **out** for the same night. You try to **get out of** the first date.

2. You **find out** that your spouse is infertile. You really want children of your own and cannot **accept adoption**. You leave your spouse.

3. Your favorite sister is **engaged to** marry a man who, in your opinion, is **bad news**. She is in love. You try to talk her **out of it**.

4. You have a serious long-distance romance in your country. To relieve **loneliness**, you start a romantic **friendship** locally. You **bring up** your commitment to the local person.

5. Your teenage daughter is dating a man of another **race**. You try to get them to **break off** their relationship.

6. In order to **marry** someone you love, you must **give up** your **religion** and change to theirs. You do it.

7. You give your mate a gift **worth** $200; then you **break up** a month **later**. You ask **for it back**.

8. You've been **going out with** a person who loves you much more than you love them. You've been **up front** about your feelings but your mate doesn't care. You end the **relationship** now in order to **spare** them a greater **hurt** later.

Answers for Follow up: Phrasal Verbs

call up
ask out
get out of
find out
talk out of
bring up
break off
give up
break up
ask for it back
go out with
be up front

Cheating in College

Partial Dictation ❀ page 28 *(CD 1, track 13)*

1. Cheating in the classroom isn't just about **copying** someone's paper or writing answers on a **crib sheet**. With the **Internet**, cheating has gone **high tech**.

2. **Hundreds** of web sites offer **term** papers, class notes, and exams. Students may pay **up to $350** for a research paper bought through the Internet.

3. **Plagiarism** is the most common form of cheating, and university professors admit that it is **hard to catch**. It depends **on the vigilance** of faculty members and a certain **degree of luck**.

4. More than **75%** of 2000 students from **21** colleges nationwide **admitted to cheating** last year.

5. Experts say that most students cheat because of **grade pressure**.

6. **Research** on college cheating shows that men and women **equally** admitted to **academic** dishonesty; business and **engineering** majors were most likely to cheat, **compared with** other majors.

7. Colleges are doing more **to prevent** cheating, and universities work with international students who come from **cultures** that allow **citing** another person's work **without quotation** marks or footnotes.

8. At some schools, possible **punishment for cheating** includes **expulsion**, but most professors simply give the student an **F in the course**.

Don't Be Fooled!

Partial Dictation ❧ page 30 *(CD 1, track 14)*

1. Mary Jones was born on December 27th, **yet** her birthday is always **in the summer**. How can this be?

    Answer: She's from a country south of the equator.

2. Frank was walking down Main Street when it started to **rain**. He did not have an umbrella and he wasn't wearing a hat. His clothes **were soaked**, yet not a hair on his head **got wet**. How could this happen?

    Answer: He is bald.

3. There is an **ancient invention** still used in parts of the world today that **allows** people to see through **walls**. What is it?

    Answer: A window.

4. A taxi driver took a group of **passengers** to the train station. The station is **normally** an hour away, but with terrible traffic, it took a full hour and **a half**. On the return trip, the traffic was still as **heavy** and yet it took only **90** minutes. Why?

    Answer: 90 minutes is the same as one and a half hours.

5. Do they have a fourth of July **in England**?

   Answer: Yes, but it's not a holiday.

6. Some months have **30** days; others have 31 days. How many have **28** days?

   Answer: All of them.

7. What five-letter word becomes **shorter** when you add **two letters** to it?

   Answer: Short.

8. A farmer had **fifteen horses**. **All but nine** died. How many did he have left?

   Answer: nine.

9. A woman from New York **married** ten different men from that city, yet she didn't **break any laws**. None of the men **died** and she **never divorced**. How was this possible?

   Answer: The woman was a minister.

10. Which one of the following words **does not belong** with the others and why? Father, Aunt, Sister, **Cousin**, Mother, Uncle

    Answer: Cousin. All the others refer to a specific sex.

Riddles: 1. d   2. a   3. b   4. c

What Used To Be

Partial Dictation ✾ page 31 *(CD 1, track 15)*

Part A

1. Before **electricity**, people used to . . .
2. The country that is now called **Thailand** . . .
3. Before **word processors**, people used to . . .
4. **Millions** of years ago . . .
5. Before doctors became **licensed, barbers** used to . . .
6. In many **ancient** and not so ancient cultures . . .
7. Before the car was **invented**, people used to . . .
8. The country that **used to be** called Ceylon . . .
9. People used to think that **potatoes** . . .
10. Before **television**, people used to . . .

Part B

♦ Before electricity, people used to read by candlelight.
♦ The country that is now called Thailand used to be called Siam.
♦ Before word processors, people used to use typewriters.
♦ Millions of years ago, dinosaurs used to roam the earth.
♦ Before doctors became licensed, barbers used to perform some operations.
♦ In many ancient and not so ancient cultures, people used to have slaves.
♦ Before the car was invented, people used to travel by horse.
♦ The country that used to be called Ceylon is now called Sri Lanka.
♦ People used to think that potatoes were poisonous.
♦ Before television, people used to read more.

Facts about Drinking

Partial Dictation ❀ page 33 *(CD 1, track 16)*

> *Note to teachers:* The legal drinking age is 21 in all states.

1. Some people can drink a lot without **ever getting** drunk.

   Answer: False. Depending on many factors, the reaction to alcohol among drinkers varies. However, people who drink large quantities of alcohol without showing much reaction have often built up a tolerance to it. This is a typical symptom of alcohol addiction. The brain is still affected; reaction times are still erratic, and judgment is impaired. For example, when a driver has been drinking, other cars may seem to be farther away than they actually are.

2. Approximately 40% of **fatal** highway accidents are **alcohol related**.

   Answer: True.

3. **Switching drinks** will make you drunker than staying with one kind of alcohol.

   Answer: False. Switching drinks can make you sick but not drunker. What causes an adverse reaction to alcohol is drinking too much, not the type of alcohol.

4. You can **coat the stomach** with milk or food to slow down the rate of intoxication.

   Answer: True.

5. The best way to **sober up** is to drink coffee and take a cold shower.

   Answer: False. If you drink coffee, you'll be awake but drunk. If you take a cold shower, you'll be clean but drunk. The best way is to sit and wait because the body metabolizes ½ ounce of pure alcohol an hour, and there is no way to speed up this process.

6. **Safety** experts say that one out of every two Americans will **be victimized by** a drunk driver.

   Answer: True.

7. A person **can overdose** on alcohol.

   Answer: True. There are about 1000 recorded alcohol overdose deaths a year; many are college students.

8. It is easy **to spot** an alcoholic.

   Answer: False. Nearly 10% of the population has a drinking problem. Ten million people in the U.S. are dependent on alcohol; many hold responsible jobs and are raising families. 40% are college graduates. However, an alcoholic's life expectancy is shortened by 10-12 years.

9. Drinking during pregnancy can affect the **unborn child**.

   Answer: True.

10. Most alcoholics are **middle-aged** or older.

    Answer: False. The highest proportion of drinking problems occur with men in their early 20s. Among those age groups surveyed by the National Survey on Drug Abuse [ages 12 to 17, 18 to 25, and 26 and over], abuse was most prevalent among those 18-25.

11. Children of alcoholics are **more likely** to develop alcoholism.

    Answer: True. Research indicates that sons have a one in three chance of developing alcoholism because, like diabetes, it is a genetic disease.

12. **Binge drinking** is defined as five drinks **within an hour** for men and **four** drinks within an hour for women.

    Answer: True. Binge drinking on college campuses is most common in the freshman year – in the 18-25 age group.

13. A **heavy drinker** is someone who drinks **four to five** drinks every night.

    Answer: True. *To the teacher:* Some students may dispute this because they come from cultures where drinking four to five drinks every night is common. In such cultures, alcoholism and heavy drinking are often common, although some individuals may be less affected by four to five drinks when heavy drinking is a regular habit over many years.

14. All drinkers are **drug users**.

    Answer: True. Alcohol is defined as a drug by the American Medical Association [the AMA] and the World Health Organization. It is a central nervous system depressant.

15. **Underage drinkers** account for 25% of the alcohol consumed in the United States.

    Answer: True.

Nutrition Quiz

Partial Dictation ❀ page 35 *(CD 1, track 17)*

1. Low-fat milk has more **calcium than whole** milk.

   Answer: True. When fat is removed from milk, other nutrients, including calcium and phosphorus, become more concentrated.

2. Multivitamin pills can give you **extra energy**.

   Answer: False. Vitamins don't provide energy. Burning calories provides energy. Calories come from carbohydrates, proteins, fats, and alcohol.

3. It's better to eat a **larger lunch** and a smaller dinner.

   Answer: True. Calories consumed early in the day have more time to get burned off completely than calories consumed near bed time.

4. People who do not eat meat, chicken, or fish are **not as healthy as** those who do.

   Answer: False. Vegetarians who eat a balanced diet of protein, carbohydrates, and fat are just as healthy.)

5. Fresh vegetables are always **more nutritious than** frozen.

   Answer: False. Fresh vegetables tend to lose their nutrients once they're picked, and the longer they sit, the more they lose. Frozen vegetables, if they're kept frozen, hold on to their vitamins.

6. If you want to make one **change** in your diet, it is better to eat three balanced meals a day, **cutting down** on **snacking** .

   Answer: True. Snack foods are typically high in calories, bad fats, chemical additives, and highly processed ingredients. Snacking on raw vegitables and fruit can be part of a healthy diet.

7. A glass or two of wine **or beer** will help you sleep well.

   Answer: False. Drinking alcohol will allow you to get to sleep easily, but sleep is sometimes interrupted at two or three in the morning.

8. **Laughter** helps keep you in good **condition**.

   Answer: True. Your ability to find humor can prolong your life.

9. When you're **on a diet**, it's better to drink white wine **than red**.

   Answer: False. It makes no difference; so choose the wine you like. A six-ounce glass of red or white wine contains about 130 calories.

10. You've been asked to **serve the steak**. A good serving size would be **the same size as** a deck of playing cards.
    Answer: True. For meat, fish, and poultry, the experts recommend a three-ounce portion, about the size of a deck of cards. As a rule of thumb, a four-ounce piece cooks down to three ounces.

11. Butter contains **more fat than margarine**.

    Answer: False. A tablespoon of either butter or margarine contains 100 calories

12. Women who eat at least **five** servings of fruits and vegetables **daily** reduce their **risk** of diabetes by **40%**.

    Answer: True.

How's Your Mental Health?

Partial Dictation ❀ page 36 *(CD 1, track 18)*

The Surgeon General of the United States recently **reported** that **one** in **five** Americans suffers from a **mental** illness. Although some may feel this is overstated, imagine that:

♦ **One** in **five** women will experience **clinical** depression in their lives, as will **one** in **seven** men.

♦ Eight to twelve percent of the population experiences a significant **anxiety disturbance**.

♦ **One** in **twenty** children has attention deficit hyperactivity disorder (ADHD).

♦ One percent of the population has **manic** depression or bipolar illness.

♦ **One** percent of the population has schizophrenia.

Through education and information it is important to be able to look at depression, anxiety, ADHD, and sleep **disorders** not as **weaknesses** but rather as real and medically based illnesses. Considering mental health problems to be **non-medically** based means that far too many will go unrecognized and **untreated**.

The **most common** mental illness is depression. Different forms of depression **range** from short-term, low mood after a **stressful** life experience to an **ongoing** form of depression linked to decreased energy, interest, and **concentration** along with changes in appetite and sleep – called **major depression**.

Depression may also take place in women following **childbirth** as well as in people during certain **seasons** of the year. Being unable to perform at work, having little wish to **socialize**, and becoming **distanced** from family members may all take place during depression. Depression very much needs to be viewed as a **medical** illness and not as a weakness. Recognizing and treating depression not only **enhances** life but also **saves** lives.

Note to teachers:

If this is a topic that your students would like to know more about and if your school has a psychology department, a professor may be willing to come and talk to the class, or perhaps someone from a counseling center can be interviewed by the class. You can also check out: www.askpsychmd.com/index.htm

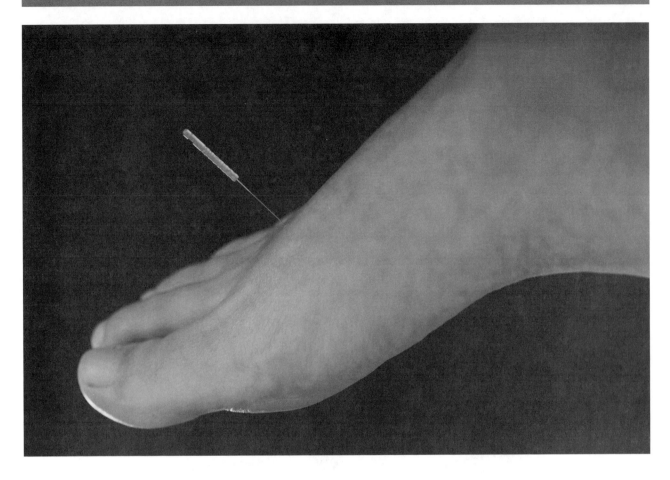

Alternative Medicine

Partial Dictation ❀ page 39 *(CD 1, track 19)*

Not long ago, the idea of treating pain with acupuncture or hypnosis would have **raised many an eyebrow** within the medical mainstream. **But now a growing number of hospitals** are offering patients alternative or complementary therapies **combined with traditional medicine**.

A big reason for the trend **is consumer demand**. A Harvard study reported **that Americans made 629 million visits** to alternative practitioners **compared with 386 million visits** to primary care doctors, spending $27 billion (a good part of it **out of pocket**) on alternative treatments.

Proponents say complementary techniques, particularly mind-body therapies, **offer many benefits**. They are non-invasive and have **no side effects**. And they tap into the healing power of the mind.

Chinese New Year

Partial Dictation ❀ page 40 *(CD 1, track 20)*

In feudal times, the Chinese believed that the eve of the New Year marked the Kitchen God's departure to heaven **in order to report on the household**. To welcome the Kitchen God **back to the home** in the New Year, each family feasted and performed a "spring-cleaning." The spring festival symbolized **a fresh start** and the earth's seasonal return to life.

"We serve **special dishes** that are auspicious for the New Year," Danny Woo, the manager at the Jumbo Seafood Restaurant in **Chinatown**, says. He is planning an **eight-course special dinner**, because eight in Chinese **is a lucky number**, since it sounds like the word "**prosper**."

Chicken and fish are cooked only in their whole form to represent a year **that starts without missing pieces**.

One traditional Chinese **recipe** for the New Year is Clams in Black Bean **Sauce**, because their **shells** resemble Chinese coins, which **symbolize prosperity**. Another **traditional** recipe is Good Luck Dumplings.

Independence Day

Partial Dictation 1 ❀ page 42 *(CD 1, track 21)*

1. France	a. July 4, 1776
2. United States of America	b. **September 7, 1822**
3. Brazil	c. **July 1, 1867**
4. Australia	d. **July 14, 1789**
5. Canada	e. **January 26, 1901**

Answers: France, d   Australia, e
             U.S.A., a   Canada, c
             Brazil, b

Partial Dictation 2 ❀

In this dictation you will hear about some of the ways the U.S. celebrates its birthday. **July 4**, the anniversary of the day the Declaration of Independence was signed, is a day in the United States **that everyone looks forward to**. About a week before the celebration, you will see small and large flags flying, and stores beginning to display **red**, **white**, and **blue decorations**.

In almost every little town across the country, there is a parade. People line the route **cheering and waving little flags**. The parade often begins with a line of **antique cars** dating from the nineteen twenties and thirties, followed by **old soldiers** marching and playing patriotic songs like *Yankee Doodle Dandy*. Even **in the age of** dazzling technology, Americans like to **maintain the tradition** of an old-fashioned parade.

In the afternoon, friends and family will gather for a **picnic or** barbecue. At one time, fresh salmon and fresh peas were part of a **traditional menu**, but the **barbecue** lends itself to chicken, steaks, and hot dogs, **all-time American favorites**.

Everyone waits for dark, **when the fireworks begin**. Most large cities have extravagant concerts and firework displays. In Boston, on the Esplanade by the Charles River, **350,000 plus people** will gather to watch and hear the Boston Pops. Some of the crowd **will have gotten up** at 6:00 a.m. to get good seats for this great show. The crowd will **sing along** to the well-known songs, and a popular star will read the Declaration of Independence while **the orchestra plays** in the background. The last piece, Tchaikovsky's *1812 Overture*, will include real cannons firing. This is the traditional ending, and the crowd cheers as the orchestra plays **its last notes**. Finally the moment arrives, and you can hear the crowd's oohs and aahs as the sensational half-hour of fireworks **begins to light up the sky** with red, white, and blue shells that burst **and then float gently down to earth**.

Natural Disasters

Partial Dictation ❀ page 44 *(CD 1, track 22)*

1. An epidemic in Nigeria in **1991** killed **10,391** people. What is the continent?
2. A **volcano** in Colombia, South America in **1985** killed **21,800** people.
3. In 2005, in the **United States**, **Hurricane** Katrina killed 1,836 people. Name the continent.
4. A tsunami in **Indonesia** in **2004** killed **110,229** people. Name the continent.
5. In China, a **flood** killed **3,700,000** people in 1931. Name the continent.
6. In **India** in **1967**, a drought killed **half a million** people.
7. 143,000 people died in an **earthquake** in **Japan** in **1923**. Name the continent.
8. In **1991**, Bangladesh was hit by a tropical **cyclone,** one of the deadliest in history. **139,000** people died. Name the continent.

Answers:

	Disaster	*Country*	*Continent*	*Year*	*# Killed*
1.	epidemic	Nigeria	Africa	1991	10,391
2.	volcano	Colombia	South America	1985	21,800
3.	hurricane	United States	North America	2005	1,836
4.	tsunami	Indonesia	Asia	2004	110,229
5.	flood	China	Asia	1931	3,700,000
6.	drought	India	Asia	1967	500,000
7.	earthquake	Japan	Asia	1923	143,000
8.	cyclone	Bangladesh	Asia	1991	139,000

Discussion Responses

1. AIDS
2. volcanoes in Italy, Caribbean, Iceland
3. earthquakes on land or in the ocean; Thailand, Malaysia
4. Most Asian countries experience earthquakes.
5. Hurricane warnings alert residents of the U.S. to evacuate, and there is generally a safe place for them to go for shelter.
6. The 1991 cyclone in Bengladesh was deadly because the country is low, flat, poor, and heavily populated.

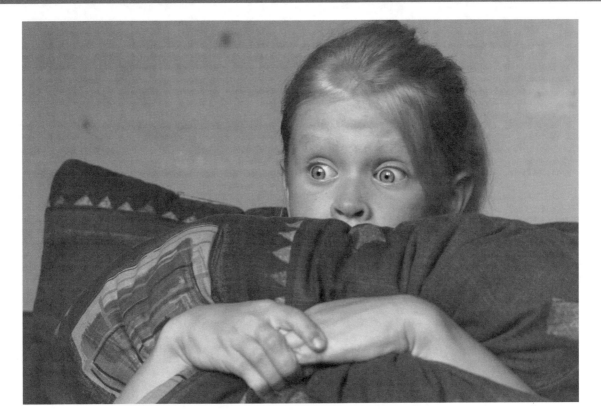

Scary Movies

Partial Dictation ❦ page 45 *(CD 1, track 23)*

Why would anyone voluntarily **sit and watch** a **two-hour movie** filled with **fear, disgust**, and **terror**? Why would anyone pay **to do this**? How could it be **enjoyable**?

Theories about **human behavior** tell us that humans try to pursue **pleasure** and **avoid pain. However**, psychologists give **two reasons** for why we enjoy **watching scary movies.**

The first is that the person is not **actually afraid** of the movie but excited by it. **The second** is that viewers are willing to endure the terror **in order to** enjoy the very happy **sense of relief** at the end.

Some of the scariest movies in English of all time are *Psycho* (**1960**), *The Shining* (**1980**), *The Silence of the Lambs* (**1991**), as well as series like *Halloween* and *Halloween II.*

Family Reunion

Partial Dictation ✦ page 47 *(CD 1, track 24)*

The Clarks were **looking forward to** June 20th, when their **six** sons, and their sons' wives and children, were coming to their Utah home for a **family reunion**. Everyone was **due** to arrive by **June 19**. Each couple had **one**, **two**, or **three** children. From the following clues, can you match the sons with their wives, determine how many children each couple had, **deduce** their time of **arrival**, and **figure out** where each family lived?

1. One couple **crossed** no state or national borders in **getting to** the homecoming.

2. The couples **arrived June 19** at **8 a.m., 10 a.m., noon, 2 p.m., 3 p.m.**, and **5 p.m.**

3. The couples from **Germany** and **Japan have** the same number of children.

4. George **has** only one child, a boy. Eileen has only two girls, and Carol **has** only one girl.

5. The son from **Texas arrived** at **10 a.m.**

6. Pat, who hails from Wyoming, **has** three children and did not arrive either first or last.

7. Frank **flew in** from **Germany** and **arrived** after **noon**, two hours after his brother from Japan.

8. Bert and Bob don't **have** the same number of children. The son from Texas **has** one **less** child than the son from Wyoming. The son from Arizona **has** one more child than Frank.

9. Wendy **arrived** after Jill, who **arrived** after Linda. But Linda **arrived** before Eileen, who **arrived** before **noon**.

10. Keith **drove** all night and **arrived** before **10 a.m.** with his three hungry children.

11. Bert **packed** his wife and two children into the car that morning and **arrived** three hours after Frank.

Solution:

> Keith and Linda from Utah arrived at 8 a.m. with three children.
> Ron and Eileen arrived from Texas at 10 a.m. with two children.
> George and Jill arrived from Japan at 12 noon with one child.
> Frank and Carol arrived from Germany at 2 p.m. with one child.
> Bob and Pat arrived from Wyoming at 3 p.m. with three children.
> Bert and Wendy arrived from Arizona at 5 p.m. with two children.

Tall, Taller, Tallest

Pair Dictation ❁ page 49 *(CD 2, track 1)*

We are growing taller. In the last 200 years growth has been dramatic. In 1760 Norwegian soldiers averaged five foot three. American soldiers drafted in World War I averaged five feet tall and 140 pounds. Today the average Californian male is five feet ten and a half inches and weighs 188 pounds.

In the Netherlands, home to the tallest population in the world, the average height of men is nearly six feet one inch.

The difference between men and women may disappear some day. Thousands of years ago men were 30% taller than women. Today height differences average 7%.

Cloning

Pair Dictation ❁ page 51 *(CD 2, track 2)*

Nicole has two cats and treasures them both. But she'd never want to double the pleasure with either one of them.

"I'm not one for cloning. I'm not for it at all," the 23-year-old said when asked her opinion about a researcher cloning a cat.

"It will lead to human cloning, and that is wrong. It's one more step. Sheep, and now this," she said in answer to a reporter's question.

She said that cloning was wrong even if it meant getting duplicates for Picky and Tornado, her two cats. "I love them to death, but I wouldn't clone them."

Jim, a 33-year-old-man, said, "Leave life alone. Cats shouldn't be cloned. Nobody should be cloned. They're spending way too much money when they could be spending it on research for something useful: find a cure for AIDS or cancer." Jim has a fox terrier named Max. "I love Max. He's 12 years old and I don't know what I would do if he died today. But when his time is up, it's up. Unfortunately, that's life."

Older Learners

Pair Dictation ❀ page 53 *(CD 2, track 3)*

For Chi-Hing nothing was more important than education. That's why at age 68 she decided to go back to school to get her high school diploma. After a year and a half Chi-Hing put on a cap and gown and received a Boston Public School Diploma in a ceremony on the eve of the Chinese New Year.

"It had always been my dream to go back to school," said Chi-Hing, "No matter what age you are, you can learn. It is never too late."

Chi-Hing moved to Boston from China in 1975. While she had been a teacher in China and Okinawa, she did not speak English nor did she have the credentials to teach in the U.S. So she went to work in a day care center and concentrated on taking care of her family. She also took Adult Education classes and English classes.

When a broken hip forced her to retire, she saw an opportunity. She had plenty of free time and her children were grown. But she worried that she was too old to go back to school.

She met a college professor who encouraged her to finish her education. "He could speak nine languages," Chi-Hing recalled. "I told him I wanted to learn, but I was too old. He encouraged me; he told me I could do it. And I did."

Food as a Second Language

Note to teachers:

If there is any chance you can make this ahead of time and bring it to class for your students to enjoy, try it! We've done it with great success!

Pair Dictation ❈ page 55 *(CD 2, track 4)*

Banana Bread
Ingredients

2 ripe bananas, mashed

2 eggs

¾ cup of flour

½ cup oil or melted margarine

1 teaspoon of baking soda and ½ teaspoon of baking powder

½ teaspoon of vanilla

¾ cup of sugar

3 tablespoons of skim milk

2/3 cup of walnuts, chopped

2/3 cup of coconut flakes (or chocolate chips)

Directions

Put the bananas in a bowl with two eggs, baking soda, and baking powder. Stir and add all other ingredients. Put in an 8 by 8 inch pan and bake at 350 degrees for 60 minutes.

Hanging Out to Dry

Pair Dictation ❧ page 57 *(CD 2, track 5)*

1. Clotheslines are one way to fight climate change using sun and wind instead of electricity. *For*

2. It indicates poverty if you put out your wash. *Against*

3. People have nice views from their windows that they'd like to keep. *Against*

4. Using a clothes dryer is a waste of energy. *For*

5. I think sheets dangling in the wind are beautiful if they're helping the environment. *For*

6. These rules are why when I look out my window I now see birds, trees, and flowers, not laundry. *Against*

7. Clothes dryers account for 6% of the total electricity consumed by U.S. households. *For*

8. Giving up dryers saves money, helps clothes last longer and smell better, conserves energy, and promotes physical fitness. *For*

Three Little Words

Pair Dictation ❀ page 59 *(CD 2, track 6)*

No television until you've done your homework. No dessert until you've cleaned up your plate. No hurry because you're not going. No way. No dishes, no movie. No time for your mother? No more arguing with your brother.

Just when you think there are no more ways to say "No," along comes "Don't." Don't screw up. Don't forget your sweater. Don't do as I do, do as I say. Don't forget to say thank you. Don't you hear what I'm saying? Don't make me say it again.

For sheer drama, there is nothing like "Stop!" Stop humming. Stop driving me crazy. Stop dating that creep. Stop acting like you're a big shot. Stop trying to be something you're not. Stop being so negative.

They're all familiar. We couldn't have survived without them. But wouldn't it be sad if No! Don't! and Stop! were the only things they learned from us ... and those three little words shaped their lives?

What's So Funny?

Pair Dictation ❀ page 61 *(CD 2, track 7)*

Joke 1

A person who speaks two languages is bilingual. A person who speaks three languages is trilingual. A person who speaks four languages is multilingual. What is a person who speaks one language? An American.

Joke 2

An English teacher wrote these words on the board: "woman without her man is nothing."

The teacher then asked the students to punctuate the words correctly.

The men wrote: "Woman, without her man, is nothing."

The women wrote: "Woman! Without her, man is nothing."

Who Would Say That?

Pair Dictation ❀ page 63 *(CD 2, track 8)*

1. It's a 2009 and in perfect condition with only 50,000 miles.
   Speaker: Used car salesman or someone trying to sell his car through an ad

2. Do you have any spare change?
   Speaker: Beggar or street person

3. We expect to be taking off in ten minutes.
   Speaker: Pilot

4. I think that Snoopy should go on a diet.
   Speaker: Veterinarian

5. Would you like to try something different this time? A perm? Or a frost?
   Speaker: Hair stylist

6. I predict that next year you'll meet the perfect man and get married.
   Speaker: Fortune teller or card reader

7. It's a home run for Reggie. Now it's tied three to three.
   Speaker: Baseball game announcer

8. May I see your driver's license and registration please?
   Speaker: Police officer

9. Open wide.
   Speaker: Dentist

10. The fine is 10 cents a day for each one that is overdue.
    Speaker: Librarian

Punctuation for the story **The Hare and the Tortoise**

One day a hare was bragging about how fast he could run. "I have never been beaten," he said. "When I put forth my full speed, I challenge anyone here to race with me."

The tortoise said quietly, "I accept your challenge."

"That is a good joke," said the hare. "I could dance around you all the way."

"Keep your boasting until I've been beaten," answered the tortoise. "Shall we race?"

"A race! What fun," said the hare.

So a course was fixed, and a starting line was made. The race began and the hare, being such a swift runner, soon left the tortoise far behind. About halfway through the course, the hare said "Oh my, I have plenty of time to beat that slow tortoise. I'll take a nap." Meanwhile, the tortoise never for a moment stopped, but went on with a slow but steady pace straight to the end of the course.

When the hare awoke from his nap, he thought it was time to get going. And off he went faster than a speeding bullet, but it was too late. He dashed up to the finish line where he met the tortoise, who was patiently awaiting his arrival. "What took you so long?" the tortoise asked.

The moral of this story is: **"Slow and steady wins the race."**

Limericks and Tongue Twisters

Note to teachers:

For best results, be sure students know the meaning of words like "squid" and "defiant."

You can also use limericks as strip stories by cutting up each line and having students work in pairs to figure out the poem. The Internet has dozens of limerick web sites.

Pair Dictation ✽ page 66 *(CD 2, track 9)*

1. There once was an old man from Nesser
    Whose knowledge grew lesser and lesser.
        It at last grew so small,
        He knew nothing at all,
    And now he's a college professor!

2. There was a young fellow named Sid
    Who loved to go fishing for squid.
        But he caught quite a giant
        Who was very defiant,
    And ate Sid all up, yes it did. (Poor kid.)

The New World Language

Pair Dictation ✸ page 68 *(CD 2, track 10)*

English is everywhere. Some 380 million people speak it as their first language, and perhaps another 250 million people speak it as their second language. A billion are learning it. By 2050 it is predicted that half of the world will be more or less proficient in it. English is the language of globalization, of international business, politics, and diplomacy.

How come? Not because English is easy. Sure, genders are simple. But the verbs tend to be irregular, the grammar bizarre, and the match between spelling and pronunciation a nightmare.

All About Weather

Pair Dictation ❀ page 70 *(CD 2, track 11)*

Joke 1

I had just moved north and was feeling apprehensive about the severity of the winters. My anxious questions about the weather brought this reply from a native. "Ma'am, we have four seasons here: early winter, midwinter, late winter, and next winter."

Joke 2

The Michaels family owned a small farm in Canada just yards away from the North Dakota border. Their land had been the subject of a minor dispute between Canada and the United States for generations. Mrs. Michaels, who had just celebrated her ninetieth birthday, lived on the farm with her son and three grandchildren. One day, her son came into her room holding a letter. "I just got some news, Mom," he said. "The government has come to an agreement with the people in Washington. They've decided that our land is really part of the United States. We have the right to approve or disapprove of the agreement. What do you think?" "What do I think?" his mother said. "Jump at it! Call them right now and tell them we accept. I don't think I could stand another one of those Canadian winters."

Answers to Cooperative Learning – All About Weather

1. Begin talking (for the first time or after an argument).

2. Talk casually.

3. You are only seeing a little bit of something. There's much more that you don't see.

4. He was drunk.

5. It's raining heavily.

6. I can't go now. Can I go another time? (This is baseball language. If it rains and they can't play, you'll get a ticket for another game.)

7. Don't spoil things for me.

8. I can succeed even if things are difficult.

9. I feel sick.

10. He convinced them even though his arguments were weak. He was not telling the truth.

11. I was amazed!

12. It was a surprise.

13. I had too much to do.

14. She was unfriendly.

15. She was very, very happy.

16. She was not very practical. She was often dreaming about other things.

Note: *See page x in the introduction for more details.*

Are You Superstitious?

Pair Dictation ❀ page 73 *(CD 2, track 12)*

A young Japanese woman named Keiko was being wheeled into operating room four when she noticed the number over the door. She began to cry softly. The nurse became concerned and asked what was wrong. Keiko was embarrassed, but explained that the Japanese character for the number four is pronounced the same as the character for the word "death." Already concerned about her health, Keiko was disturbed to be wheeled into a room labeled "death." Although she said it was just a silly superstition, Keiko was unable to let go of her fear.

The surgery went well despite the room number, but the patient suffered needless anxiety. Had the hospital personnel mentioned to Keiko that she was being scheduled for room four, her feelings might have become known in time to reschedule her surgery into a different room. Room number three, for example, would have been appropriate because "three" in Japanese characters also means "life."

All About Ice Cream

Answer to Chronological Order: 5 1 6 8 2 7 3 9 4

Pair Dictation ❀ page 76 *(CD 2, track 13)*

1. Americans consume more ice cream than any other country in the world on a per capita basis. The Australians come in second. In 1924 the average American ate eight pints a year. By 1997 that figure had jumped to 48 pints a year.

2. Vanilla is the most popular flavor in the U.S.A., getting anywhere from 20 to 29 percent of sales. Chocolate comes in a distant second with about 9 to 10% of the market.

3. One out of every five ice cream eaters share their treat with their dog or cat.

4. One of the major ingredients in ice cream is air. Without it, the stuff would be as hard as a rock. Some types of ice cream are more than 75 percent air.

5. Among the most unusual flavors of ice cream ever manufactured are avocado, garlic, azuki bean, jalapeño, and dill pickle.

6. A major invention in the late 19th century was the ice cream sundae. Its odd name comes from Sunday, but no one knows why. The biggest ice cream sundae was made in Alberta, Canada, in 1988 and weighed nearly 55,000 pounds.

Childhood

Pair Dictation ❀ page 80 *(CD 2, track 14)*

An estimated 158 million children ages 5 to 14 are engaged in child labor. This is one in six children in the world.

Millions of children work in dangerous situations. They work in mines, work with chemicals and pesticides in agriculture, and work with dangerous machinery. One example is a four-year-old tied to a rug loom to keep the child from running away.

Millions of very young girls work as domestic servants in households where they are exploited and abused. Of course, work prevents these children from going to school. Also, many children, some as young as ten, are child soldiers and are fighting in wars around the world.

Bono

Answer to Chronological Order: 4, 8, 1, 3, 7, 2, 5, 6

Dictogloss ✿ page 82 *(CD 2, track 15)*

1. Bono has been nominated for the Nobel Peace Prize three times.

2. His name, Bono, comes from *bono vox* which means "Good Voice" in Latin.

3. He has spent a lot of time, money, and energy fighting AIDS, TB, and malaria.

4. Since the 1990s he has almost always worn sunglasses on stage because of his sensitive eyes.

5. Bono is admired not only as a singer and songwriter but also as a very good human being.

Help Bono Help Haiti: highlights of concert on YouTube
Buy the album/all proceeds to Haiti: www.cmt.com/haiti
♦ **www.unicefusa.org/work/emergencies/Haiti** ♦
♦ **www.helphaitinow.org** ♦ **www.hope-for-haiti.org** ♦

Ten Interesting Questions

Dictogloss ❀ page 84 *(CD 2, track 16)*

1. Which sex has an easier life in your culture, male or female?

2. If you saw someone cheating on a test, what would you do?

3. Would you ever consider taking a week-long vacation alone?

4. Have you ever taken a sick day from school or work when you weren't sick?

5. Which would you rather have, a nice teacher or a strict teacher?

6. Do you have any specific long-term goals?

7. Are you more interested in international, national, state, or local news?

8. Would you rather become extremely rich as a result of luck or hard work?

9. Would you rather play a game with someone more, or less, talented than you?

10. Would you like to be famous some day?

The Rise of Wives

Dictogloss ❀ page 86 *(CD 2, track 17)*

1. This report focused on U.S.-born men and women aged 30 to 44.

2. In nearly a third of marriages today, the wife is better educated than her husband.

3. While most men still earn more than women, wives are now the primary breadwinner in 22% of couples.

4. The shift in roles means that more men are taking on more housework responsibilities.

5. Career women today are more likely to choose men who support a more equal marital relationship.

6. Unmarried men with college degrees made income gains of 15%, but unmarried women with degrees gained 28%.

Marriage and Divorce

Partial Dictation ✿ page 87 *(CD 2, track 18)*

1. People with a college degree **tend to marry later** and stay married.
2. Among married women ages 25 to **44** with a college degree, 15 **out of 1000** divorced within a year, compared with **30** out of 1000 women with just a **high school diploma**.
3. People's average age at their first marriage **increased** to **24.9** years for women and **27.1** for men.
4. In the 1950s and 1960s the **average age** for women to marry was **20** and for men it was **24**.
5. Divorce is least likely to **occur** among **Asians** and most likely to occur among **African-Americans**.

Dictogloss ✿

1. About 9 out of 10 Americans are expected to marry at least once in their lifetime.
2. Half of first marriages end in divorce, but three in four will probably remarry.
3. First marriages that end in divorce typically last about eight years.
4. The earlier people are married, the more likely they are to get divorced.
5. Among younger men, having an older wife is becoming more common.

Follow up Prediction Dictation:

Dear Advisor:

My parents **are** divorced. I live **with** my mother. I spend two weekends **a** month with my dad and one month in **the** summer with him. I love my **Dad**, but he has remarried, and I don't really **like** his new wife, Amy. My father is **really** nice to me and takes **me** places, but Amy sort of resents me and I feel **uncomfortable** around her.

Now that **I'm** 15, I would rather **spend** more time at home with my friends. I also **want** to get a part-time **job** this summer. Do you think **my** father will be **hurt** if I don't visit him this **summer**? What do you think I should do?

Joey in Jamestown

Obesity

Dictogloss ❀ page 89 *(CD 2, track 19)*

1. Some say that obesity kills as many as 325,000 every year.

2. Researchers are surprised at how fast Americans are gaining weight.

3. Some health problems from obesity are heart attacks, high blood pressure, and diabetes.

4. If obese people ate 200 fewer calories a day, they would be 20 pounds lighter in a year.

5. Drugs taken for certain mental illnesses can cause huge weight gains.

Television

Answer to Chronological Order: 3, 1, 5, 7, 10, 2, 6, 9, 4, 8

Dictogloss ❁ page 90 *(CD 2, track 20)*

1. Half of American homes have three or more TVs.

2. "Sesame Street," a popular children's program, began in 1969.

3. Watching TV has been linked to obesity in children.

4. TV is now on buses and planes, in elevators, and in airport lobbies.

5. The average person watches an average of 4 hours and 35 minutes of TV a day.

6. Because of progress in electricity and transmitters, by the 1990s half the world could watch television.

AIDS

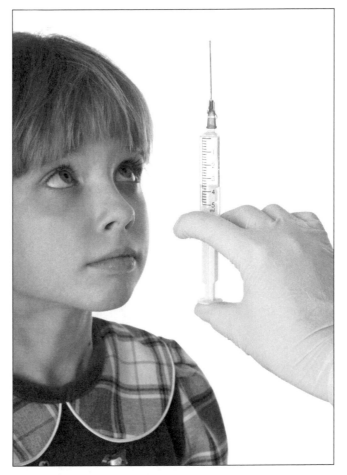

This nine-year-old child is being treated for AIDS.

Answers to Quiz: 1. d   2. a   3. d   4. d

Dictogloss ❀ page 92 *(CD 2, track 21)*

1. AIDS is now a pandemic.

2. You can't tell by looking at someone if he or she has AIDS.

3. Worldwide, 15- to 24-year-olds account for half of all new infections.

4. People can have HIV without knowing that they have it, because they don't have any symptoms.

5. About 1.1 million Americans are infected with the HIV virus, and a quarter of them do not know it.

Idioms for Test Takers

Dictogloss ❀ page 94 *(CD 2, track 22)*

1. I blew it.

2. I screwed up.

3. I aced the test.

4. I'm a basket case.

5. I'm really uptight.

6. The test was a no-brainer.

7. I hit the books last night.

8. It was a piece of cake.

Discussion answers:

1 1 2 3 6 8
2 4 5

Answers for **Cooperative Learning – Working with Idioms**

Group 1

1. I got slowed down; delayed; confused.
2. He's arrogant; thinks he knows all the answers.
3. She's super smart; a nerd.
4. We all have similar opinions on the issue.

Group 2

1. I was prepared and excited.
2. She was very happy.
3. She took a long nap.
4. They raised their hands in the air and slapped each other's hands.

Group 3

1. She can't possibly pass the course.
2. He needed to talk and complain about it.
3. They punished him; probably expelled him.
4. She is very busy.

Group 4

1. The teacher gave an unexpected quiz.
2. I heard a rumor that everyone passed the test.
3. He went to bed and fell asleep instantly.
4. She was expecting to get an A.

Make a Difference, Be a Volunteer!

Note Taking ❀ page 96 *(CD 2, track 23)*

Answer to Chronological or Logical Order: 4 6 7 1 3 2 5 8

1. Josh Ryan, 48, of Bandera, Texas, invested $10,000,000 from his pro-basketball career to open Ryan Ranch, a home to 1300 young adults, many of whom have been abused or abandoned.

2. Leon Goldberg, 68, of Detroit, Michigan, kept his 3000 workers on the payroll after a fire destroyed his textile mill last year. He rebuilt the plant, and all but 400 are now back on the job.

3. LaToya Jefferson, 51, of Milltown, Florida, is a volunteer at Paula's Place, a homeless shelter for African-American women. She has been there to cook for five hours a day for ten years and remains friends with the women, even after they leave.

4. Addie May Carlson, 75, of Oakdale, California, has been running low-cost summer camps for disabled children for five years. She accepts no salary.

5. Bob Dean, 36, of Chicago, Illinois, grew up in a poor neighborhood and knows what it's like to be on probation. One day he showed up at the courthouse and offered to help kids in trouble. He's been volunteering for 12 years, sometimes 30 hours a week. "I've seen a lot of pain," he says.

6. Lena Chin, 52, of New York City, arrived from China in 1986 and soon began volunteering several days a week in her city's Chinatown to help Asian immigrants whose inability to speak and read English makes it impossible for them to fill out the complicated forms required for health benefits.

Birthdays around the World

Note Taking ❀ page 99 *(CD 2, track 24)*

Germany

Germans take birthdays seriously, sometimes receiving a half-day vacation from work. Flowers and wine are common gifts.

Japan

The birthday child wears entirely new clothes to mark the occasion. Certain birthdays are more important than others. For example, the "coming of age" birthday at age 20 is considered one of the most important. Ages 60, 70, 79, 88, and 99 are also significant.

Denmark

A flag is flown outside a window to designate that someone who lives in that house is having a birthday. Presents are placed around the child's bed while they are sleeping so they will see them immediately upon awakening.

England, Canada, Australia, and New Zealand

When you reach 100 or 105 years of age, you may receive a letter from the Queen. (In the U.S. when you reach 100, you receive a letter from the President).

China

Age 30 is considered becoming an adult, and there is usually quite a celebration. Birthdays are traditionally celebrated for adults who have reached at least 60 years of age. Lo mein noodles are often served.

Mexico

The piñata, usually made out of papier maché and in the form of an animal, is filled with goodies and hung from the ceiling. Children take turns hitting the piñata so candy and small toys spill out for everyone to share. Also, when a daughter is 15, the birthday is celebrated with a special mass in her honor. A party is given to introduce her to everyone as a young woman. The father dances a waltz with her.

Answers for **Cooperative Learning – Birthdays** (*a few examples*)
Group 1

1. Argentina, Albania, Armenia, Austria, Australia, Azerbaijan, Afghanistan, Algeria, Angola, Andorra
2. Athens, Amsterdam, Ankara, Almaty, Alexandria, Asunción
3. Atlanta, Augusta, Albany, Austin, Annapolis
4. *(teacher to be aware of answers)*

Group 2

1. Colombia, Chile, Costa Rica, Cuba, China, Canada, Cambodia, Chad, Cameroon, Central African Republic, Croatia, Czech Republic, Cyprus, Cape Verde, Congo
2. Copenhagen, Calcutta, Cairo, Canton (Guangzhou), Cologne, Caracas, Capetown
3. Cheyenne, Columbus, Columbia, Carson City, Charleston
4. *(teacher to be aware of answers)*

Group 3

1. Mexico, Morocco, Mali, Mauritania, Mozambique, Madagascar, Malawi, Moldova, Malaysia, Malta, Monaco, Montenegro, Macedonia, Mongolia, Myanmar, Maldives, Micronesia
2. Moscow, Manila, Montevideo, Mexico City, Melbourne, Munich, Mumbai, Montreal
3. Madison, Miami, Minneapolis, Montpelier, Montgomery
4. *(teacher to be aware of answers)*

Group 4

1. Saudi Arabia, Syria, Singapore, Scotland, Spain, Switzerland, Slovakia, Slovenia, Sweden, Samoa, Surinam, Sri Lanka, Sudan, Sierra Leone, Somalia, South Africa, Swaziland, Senegal, San Marino, Serbia, South Korea
2. Stockholm, Seville, St. Petersburg, Salzburg, Seoul, Sapporo, Sarajevo, Sofia
3. Sacramento, Salem, Santa Fe, St. Paul, Salt Lake City
4. *(teacher to be aware of answers)*

The People's Court

Note Taking ❀ page 101 *(CD 2, track 25)*

Case 1

Two women gave their landlord an $800 security deposit before moving into their apartment. When they moved out three years later, the landlord refused to return the $800. He said that the women left holes in the walls from hanging pictures and stains on the carpet. The women claimed the slight damage was from normal wear and tear of apartment living. In court the landlord produced bills totaling $1500 for painting and cleaning he had done.

Case 2

Your local dry cleaners lost your winter coat, valued at $500, but refused to pay the full amount because they say it's only worth $200.

Case 3

The auto shop repaired something you didn't request, charged you for it, and refused to release the car until you paid for it with a certified check or cash. You protested, but needed your car, so you paid. You demand the $525 back.

Case 4

The 12-year-old kid next door hit a baseball through your window. His parents say it's his responsibility to pay for it. But his weekly allowance is $4.00, and it would take three years to collect the full amount.

You Be The Judge

Note Taking ❀ page 102 *(CD 2, track 26)*

Case 1 – New York

A driver who was racing down the street at 100 miles per hour crashed into a limousine carrying a wedding party. Instantly killed were the groom, age 27, and his brother, 29, who was the best man. The bride, age 24, died 18 days later without knowing of her husband's death. The driver of the car that killed them was sentenced to three years in prison.

Case 2 – Texas

A man got into an argument with a police officer and bit off part of the officer's ear. The man was sentenced to 10 years in prison.

Case 3 – Massachusetts

A 14-year-old girl was raped by a 38-year-old man. She said that her life would never be the same again. The judge told her to "get over it" and sentenced the man to six months in prison.

Plastics Alert

Note Taking ❈ page 103 *(CD 2, track 27)*

According to a recent news article, we should not be using plastic containers when heating our food in the microwave. This applies especially to foods that contain fat. Researchers say that the combination of fat, high heat, and plastics releases dioxins into the food and ultimately into the cells of the body. Because dioxins are highly toxic, doctors recommend using glass or ceramic containers for heating food.

Short Business Decisions

Note Taking ❀ page 104 *(CD 2, track 28)*

Situation 1

Julia is the manager of Robil's Ice Cream Café. In spite of the weak economy, people seem to be eating more ice cream, and business is up by 20%. Julia needs to hire one more employee to work nights and on weekends. Julia's former high school friend, Margaret, needs a job and applies for the position. She has never worked in an ice cream store before. Previously she had been a clerk in an office. Richard has also applied for the job. He has had experience working in a similar store and has excellent references. Who should Julia hire?

Situation 2

Charles, owner and president of the Welland Construction Company, has the opportunity to get a contract to build an addition to an elementary school. The contract is for two and a half million dollars. The problem for Charles is that the official who will make the final decision has asked for a payback of $15,000 in return for giving him the contract. Charles has never faced this situation before. What should he do?

Situation 3

Jack is the CEO of an international bank. There is an opening for an overseas position. The person who is chosen would become a senior executive and earn a large salary. After interviewing nine employees Jack is convinced that Louise, who has worked for the bank for five years, is the best candidate. Louise is 35 years old. She has a husband who is a technical writer and works from home, where he helps to take care of their two small children. She is a valuable member of the company and has indicated that she might leave if she doesn't get the job. The problem is that she might not be well received in the country she is going to, where there are very few women in high positions and the bank could lose business. What should Jack do?

Hold the Pickles, Hold the Lettuce

Note to teachers: Accept any logical or grammatically correct answers.

Prediction Dictation ❀ page 106 *(CD 2, track 29)*

What is perhaps **most** astonishing about America's fast **food** business is just how successful it **has** become: what began in the 1940s as a handful of hot dog and hamburger stands in Southern California **has** spread across the land to become a $110 billion industry. **According to** Eric Schlosser, the author of *Fast Food Nation*, **Americans** now spend more on **fast food than** they spend on higher **education**, personal computers, **computer** software, or new cars, or on movies, books, videos, and recorded music combined. Mr. Schlosser writes that on any given day in the **United States** about one quarter of the adult population visits a fast food **restaurant**, and that the typical **American** now consumes approximately three hamburgers and four orders of French **fries** every week.

"An estimated one of **every** eight workers in the United States has at some time been employed **by** McDonald's," he adds, and the company hires more **people** than any other American organization, public or **private**.

As fast **food** franchises from McDonald's to Pizza **Hut** to KFC go global, this dynamic has assumed international flavor. In Brazil, Mr. Schlosser reports, McDonald's **has become** the nation's largest private employer. **Classes** at McDonald's Hamburger University in Oak Park, Illinois, are now taught in 20 different **languages**, and a Chinese anthropologist notes that all the **children** in a primary school in Beijing recognized an image of Ronald McDonald. For the **Chinese**, the anthropologist noted, McDonald's represents "Americana and the promise of modernization."

Note: KFC is now the official name of Kentucky Fried Chicken.

Answers to Follow up: Hold the Pickles, Hold the Lettuce

1. I don't want any pickles or lettuce.

2. I want to take it home. I don't want to eat it in the restaurant.

3. Don't put too much salt on the food.

4. Don't put too much salad dressing on the salad.

5. I want the inside of my meat to be pink.

6. When you fry the egg, don't turn it over; I want to see the yolk.

7. When you fry the egg, turn it over so both sides look white.

8. No milk or cream in my coffee.

9. Lots of pickles, please.

10. I'll have two pieces of chicken, a breast and a leg.

11. Please put the dressing in a little cup on the side. I'll put it on.

12. Give me everything. (For example, on a sandwich you want them to add tomatoes, lettuce, onions, pickles, olives, sprouts, hot peppers, *etc.*)

Babe Didrikson Zaharias

Note to teachers: Accept any logical or grammatically correct answers.

Prediction Dictation ❀ page 109 *(CD 2, track 30)*

When Babe Didrikson was **a** teenager in 1925, she knew her life's ambition. "My goal was to be the **greatest** athlete who ever lived," she said.

Her parents **were** hard-working immigrants **from** Norway, and Babe grew up in a tough working-class environment that helped shape her independent **and** self-reliant spirit. A tomboy, she was strong and driven **to** assert herself. In elementary school **she** was dubbed "Babe" after Babe Ruth because of her athletic **ability** on the baseball field.

In school, she dominated **every** sport she tried: volleyball, tennis, baseball, swimming, and especially basketball, which was very **popular** among young women at the time. At **age** 18, she was recruited to **join** a company's professional basketball team, where she quickly **became** the star. Soon after, she amazed audiences **in** many track and field events as well. In the 1932 Olympics she won several gold **medals** for track and field.

While Babe was a natural athlete, it was **her** incredible determination that made her a champion. Her next **sport** to tackle was golf, where she **was** an unstoppable force, winning 82 tournaments **in** the 30s and 40s. She co-founded the Ladies Professional Golf Association (LPGA), a world-wide **organization**.

On the golf course she **met** George Zaharias, a Greek-American, in 1938. They married and Babe took and **used** her husband's name, but by then the Didrikson name **was** famous.

Didrikson was at **the** top of her career in the early 50s, and with all her tour winnings **and** endorsements, she was **earning** over $100,000 a year, an incredible **feat** for a woman athlete of that time. But in 1953, she faced a major **problem** she couldn't overcome – colon cancer. After the surgery, **doctors** said she'd be too weak to **play** sports, but four months later she was **back** in golf tournaments. And in 1954 she **started** winning again. She continued playing until 1955, when **unfortunately** the cancer returned. She held on for another year. Didrikson, arguably **one of the** greatest athletes of the twentieth century, **died** on September 27, 1956.

Cults on Campus

Note to teachers: Accept any logical or grammatically correct answers.

Prediction Dictation ❀ page 113 *(CD 2, track 31)*

Shawn, student at UCLA:

In the middle of my freshman year, I **was** having a tough time socially, since I broke up **with** my girlfriend and **my** roommate was always out with friends. So when this friendly-looking **guy** came up to me on campus, **he** caught me when I was in a real funk. He was very **nice** and polite, and we talked **about** campus issues and friends. After a while he **asked** me to think about coming **and** joining a group he was in where I could make some new **connections**. I decided to give it a shot. But when I was **at** the second long "meeting" I **began** to feel I was getting sucked into something I wasn't **sure** about … like they started making me feel guilty and ashamed about everything I **did**. Then they made some remarks **about** how I'd be better off limiting contact with **family** and friends. Even though I **was** feeling depressed, it didn't feel **right**. I felt a tremendous relief when I decided not to go **back**.

Karen, student at NYU:

When I arrived here, I was **really** excited about coming to a new city to **study**. It was my first time away **from** home and I was psyched to break away from my **old** life and meet new **friends**. One day **in** the cafeteria, a nice-looking guy, who I **thought** was a student, approached me and **we** got talking. At first **it** was about family and friends, **and** we really seemed **to** hit it off, but later on into **the** conversation, I figured out that he **was not** a student here. Then he started making suggestions that I **come** to his church club, where I could **make** new friends. After a half hour **I** was getting really bad vibes about the **way** he tried to latch on to me. Finally, I told **him** to get lost. When I **wrote** about this in my journal to my English professor, she **told** me that there are **about** 3,000 cults operating in the U.S. and that the fast-growing **cult**, the International Churches of Christ, **has** been banned from at least 39 colleges.

Winning in Las Vegas

Note to teachers: Accept any logical or grammatically correct answers.

Prediction Dictation ❀ page 117 *(CD 2, track 32)*

I need an unbiased person with a good set of brains to help **me** sort this out. A woman I work **with** (we're compatible friends) decided we should **take** our vacation together and **go** to Las Vegas and gamble, just for the heck of it. Nellie **and** I saved all year, and each of us **was** able to **save** $1800 for the trip. After travel and hotel expenses, we **had** just $400 left for gambling.

Nellie and I **had** a terrific time, saw some **great** shows, and ate like royalty. We lost some **money** at blackjack and the craps tables so **we** stopped and went for **the** slot machines, which we **both** love. We each had $100 left, **and** decided to **play** the one-dollar machines.

By 2:30 a.m., we **were** exhausted, and all the money we had set aside for **gambling** was gone. Nellie started to walk **back** to our rooms. I then said, "I'm going to **put** one last dollar in **and** call it quits." I stepped over to the **slot** that Nellie had been feeding all night, put in a **dollar**, and lo and behold, I hit the jackpot! The **money** was falling all over the floor, and it **seemed** like an endless stream of silver dollars was **coming** out. I counted the total, and it **came** to $1200.

Nellie **yelled**, "You have to split that with me. I fed that machine **all** night!" I replied, "When you **walked** away, it became MY machine. I don't owe you **anything**." She yelled, "What kind of **friend** are you anyway?" Well, I **realized** our friendship was at stake, and **decided** to split my winnings with Nellie. I **would** like to know, was I a fool to **do** it, or was I morally obligated **to** share my winnings? Please tell me what you **think**.

Tess in Texas

The Olympic Games

Notes to teachers: 1. Accept any logical or grammatically correct answers.

  2. The use of B.C. and A.D. may concern or confuse some students who are used to the designations B.C.E. and C.E. B.C. means Before Christ, and A.D. stands for *Anno Domini*, Latin for "in the year of Our Lord." B.C.E and C.E. refer to the Common/Current/Christian Era. All of these terms relate to the traditional date for the birth of Christ. The designation of the Common or Current Era is preferred by some people. B.C. and A.D. are the most widely understood designations in North America.

  3. John Lennon's *Imagine* is a good song to play for this unit.

Prediction Dictation ❦ page 121 *(CD 2, track 33)*

The Ancient Games

Ancient Greece gave birth to the Olympics more than 2000 years **ago** in 776 B.C. The Games ended in 394 A.D. During those 1000 years, the Ancient Games **were** festivals to honor the many gods that Greeks **worshiped**. Olympia, the town where the most powerful god, Zeus, was worshiped, **held** the first Olympics. The first Olympic Games consisted of no more than **one** foot race, but as the Games **became** more popular, other events were **added**, such as horse racing, boxing, chariot racing, and wrestling.

Young men of wealth dominated the early Games, but later, as other sports festivals became more and more popular and offered big cash **prizes** to winners, men of all **classes** of society could make sports a **full-time** career. The Olympic Games never offered cash prizes; it was the **glory** of winning that meant everything to young men ages 12 to 17.

The Modern Games

The Olympics were **revived** in 1896 and were held every four years. The Modern Games were later **divided** into the Winter and **Summer** Games. Now the Winter and Summer Games alternate every two **years**. Fewer countries and sports are represented at the Winter Games because fewer **athletes** come from countries with high mountains and snowfields. The Summer Games **attract** thousands of athletes from over 200 countries and include many more types of sports, **such as** swimming and running. Many Olympic athletes today think of the Olympics as more than just **winning** the gold, silver, or bronze **medal**. They **believe** that doing your personal best brings respect and understanding for **all** athletes playing the same game for peace **and** humanity.

Discussion Answers for **The Olympic Games**

1. *Class Contest*

Winter	**Summer**
Snowboarding	Gymnastics
Figure skating	Rowing
Curling	Beach volleyball
Bobsled	Table tennis
Ice hockey	Weight lifting
Speed skating	Wrestling
Luge	Soccer
Downhill skiing	Field hockey
	Martial arts
	Bicycling
	Horseback riding
	Fencing
	Rollerblading

2. Sports added in the past 20 years: Curling, Snowboarding, Beach volleyball

3. Top 10 medal winners in Winter Olympics in Vancouver, Canada, in 2010.

   1. Canada   2. Germany   3. United States   4. Norway

   5. South Korea   6. Switzerland   7. China   8. Sweden

   9. Austria   10. Netherlands

4. The following countries do not have a cold climate:
   Ghana and Cayman Islands

5. Chariot racing is no longer an Olympic sport.

Follow up

2014: Sochi, Russia   2016: Rio de Janeiro, Brazil

As of this printing, no other countries have been named. The contenders for 2018 are France, Germany, and South Korea.

Election Day in the U.S.A.

Answers for questions in the introduction

1. November   2. every 4 years   3. for 8 years

Note to teachers: Accept any logical or grammatically correct answers.

Prediction Dictation ❀ page 125 *(CD 2, track 34)*

In the United States, presidential **elections** are held every four years. They are always **held** on the first Tuesday after the first Monday in the month of **November**. In most states, Election Day is not a holiday from **work** or school. The president and the vice-president are **elected** for four years. Only natural-born **citizens** of the United States are **allowed** to be president. Presidents are **required** to be at least thirty-five years old.

There are two major political **parties**, the Democratic Party **and** the Republican Party. The vice-presidential **candidates** are selected by the presidential candidates. Both people are nominated by their **political** parties at national conventions several months **before** Election Day.

On Election Day, **millions** of Americans go to the polls to **vote**. Polls are **located** in schools, churches, and public buildings. Polls are **open** from early in the morning until 7:00 or 8:00 in the **evening**. Most polls use a **voting** machine. People always **vote** by secret ballot.

Today, all United States **citizens** 18 and **older** can vote if they want to. In presidential elections, **about** 50 to 60% of Americans of voting age vote. On election night the votes are tabulated by **computer**, and the winner is usually **announced** by midnight.

Note to teachers on Discussion 2

1. Column A. There are no correct answers here. Accept different opinions. Just get the students to explain why they decided on each one. The purpose is to get them to talk.

2. Column B. Answers will vary according to who is in office. Explain to students that Democrats and Republicans may both want to improve education but have different ideas on how that is done.

Learning Styles

Prediction Dictation ❀ page 128 *(CD 2, track 35)*

Here is a description of one kind of **learner**, the logical learner. These people **are** very mathematically inclined. **They** enjoy problems, particularly if they are math-related. They are similar to Mr. Spock on **Star Trek** because they are very logical, straightforward types **of** learners. They always want to know **how** things work, how things relate to one **another**, and why things are here. When they were **children**, their favorite toys were building blocks and puzzles. Many of them are now engineers.

Psychologists will give **you** a learning style inventory test to see what **kind** of a learner you **are**. Here are a **few** examples of statements that could be on these **tests**.

I prefer to fiddle with things while I listen or talk **to** people.

I prefer to **read** a map rather than listen to **people** giving me directions.

I enjoy doing more than one thing **at a** time.

Bad Hair Day

Note to teachers: Accept any logical or grammatically correct answers.

Prediction Dictation ❀ page 132 *(CD 2, track 36)*

Albert **had** grown his hair ten inches because he wanted a special hairstyle. He **went** to a hair **salon** that a **friend** had recommended and brought with **him** a photograph **from** a magazine of the style he wanted.

After the **haircut**, he was furious because the **hairdresser** had **cut** the hair on top of his **head** much **too** short. His friends made **fun** of **him**. He had to **wear** a baseball **cap** for two **months**, day and **night**. He was so **unhappy** that he went to **see** a psychiatrist. Finally he sued the **hairdresser** for ten thousand **dollars**.

You are the judge. What is your **decision**? Would you make the **hairdresser** pay Albert **ten thousand dollars**?

The Verdict

The court ruled against Albert and dismissed the case because the court held that the hair can easily be grown back.

Answers to the Idioms

1. Her hair looks terrible.
2. The movie was very scary.
3. Relax and have fun.
4. He just won. It was very close.
5. He lost all his money in the stock market.
6. You'd better save your money in case you need it later.
7. Don't tell anyone. It's a secret.
8. One bad thing has happened. Now he's waiting for another bad thing to happen.
9. She's always ready to do something or go somewhere.
10. He has decided to enter a political race and run for office.

Exercise

Prediction Dictation ❀ page 134 *(CD 2, track 37)*

Ruth Rothfarb **of** Cambridge was an elderly athlete who inspired many by competing **in** the Boston Marathon (26 miles), the Tufts 10K (10 kilometers), and other long-distance **races**. Mrs. Rothfarb, who died Wednesday at **age** 96, began running at the age of 69. She began running competitively a few **years** later.

She competed **in** several Boston marathons and Tufts 10K races as well as long-distance **races** in Atlanta, Los Angeles, New Zealand, and Thailand before her retirement **at** the age of 92. She **was** born in Russia and immigrated **to** the United **States** as a teenager in 1913. After her marriage, she worked full time maintaining a home, raising two **children**, and helping her **husband** run the family clothing business.

At the age of 67 she found herself with time on her hands after her husband died, their business was sold, and her children were **grown**. "I had to do something," she **said**. "I wasn't going to sit around doing **nothing**."

She began taking walks along the Charles River and around Fresh Pond. When the jogging craze came to her neighborhood, she picked up her speed. "If they can do it, I can **too**," she **said**. "It's simple enough. All you have to do is pick up your feet and **run**."

In 1976 she accompanied her son, Herbert, to a 10-kilometer **race**. "While everyone was warming up, I asked my **son** if they'd laugh at me if I **ran**," she said. "He said **no**. So I **did**. And I finished. It took me a long time, but I **finished**." She was 75 at the time.

At the age of 84 she was running about 10 miles a **day** and running marathons in about 5 ½ hours. "I like to get going," she said. "If I feel like doing something, I want to do it. I don't have to wait around for anybody else. I don't believe in spending afternoons just **sitting** around having tea. I do things."

Other Books from Pro Lingua

Two other books of dictations
by Catherine Sadow and Judy DeFilippo

Great Dictations (high beginner/low intermediate) and **Interactive Dictations** (intermediate). The students are given a newspaper or magazine article as a dictation; several dictation techniques are used, most involving filling in blanks in a gapped text. After checking their work with each other, they discuss the articles, and in the intermediate book they are given a writing assignment. Listening to the articles read by native speakers on CD helps build listening comprehension.

Conversation Strategies. 29 structured pair activities for developing strategic conversation skills at the intermediate level. Students learn the words, phrases, and conventions used by native speakers in the active give-and-take of everyday discourse.

Discussion Strategies. Carefully structured pair and small-group work at the advanced-intermediate level. Excellent preparation for students who will participate in academic or professional work that requires effective participation in discussions and seminars.

In My Opinion. 50 contemporary, thought-provoking topics presented in two basic photocopyable formats. Just over half of them are in the form of a questionnaire that students fill out and/or respond to orally. Then they compare responses and discuss the "gaps" between their views – what is good/bad, right/wrong, liberal/conservative, and so on. The other activities use opinion cards, 12 to a page, asking the cardholder to voice an opinion to be agreed upon or challenged by the others in the class.

Conversation Inspirations. A photocopyable collection of over 2400 conversation topics. A quick and easy source of topics to get your students talking about human nature, interpersonal relationships, and North American society. There are eight different types of activities: talks, interviews, role plays, chain stories, discussions, and three group creativity activities.

Improvisations. Photocopyable. High beginner to advanced. The two-page format is in three parts. *Getting Ideas*: The students explore the theme through brainstorming, free writing, graphic organizers, and other activities. *The Story*: The students read a short scene that leaves much to the imagination. Finally, *The Improvisation*: The students work in groups to develop the characters and the story line, and then perform it without a script.

Questions? Simply give us a call, and we'll try to help.
802-257-7779
www.ProLinguaAssociates.com